The Complete Beginners Guide to Trading

Cryptocurrency, forex, stocks, options, futures, and bonds

Table of Contents

Introduction 1

Chapter 1: An Introduction To The World Of Trading 3

    The different ways of trading 4

    Online Trading Platforms 7

    The role of a broker 9

    Broker Commissions 11

    Broker Fees 14

    Operational Hours of Trading Markets 16

    The benefits of trading 20

    The disadvantage of trading 23

    Technical analysis 28

    Fundamental analysis 31

    Types of Trade Orders 42

Chapter 2: Stocks 48

    What is the stock market? 48

    What is a stock? 49

    Why do companies issue stock? 50

    The different types of stocks 50

    What are Dividends? 52

    How to categorize companies in the stock market 54

    How are stock prices determined? 56

    The valuation of a stock 57

The Risk/Reward of a stock 58

How do traders buy and sell stocks? 59

Chapter 3: Futures **60**

What is the futures market? 60

What is a futures contract? 61

What are the different types of futures contracts? 62

How do traders buy and sell futures contracts? 63

How are future prices determined? 63

The valuation of a future contract 64

The Risk/Reward of a future contract 65

Chapter 4: Forex **68**

What is a currency pair? 68

How are currencies traded on the forex market? 70

Who controls the forex markets? 70

What are the main technical indicators used for trading on the forex market? 71

The risk/return of trading currencies using technical analysis . 72

How do traders make money trading currencies on the forex market? 75

What are the different types of orders? 76

What is a pip? 77

Why is the forex market so volatile? 77

What is High-Frequency Trading? 78

Chapter 5: Bonds **80**

What is a Bond? 81

How are bonds issued? 82

The different types of bonds 83

The maturity date of bonds 85
The rating of bonds 85
The yield of a bond 86
What factors affect the price of a bond? 87
The Risk/Reward of a bond 89
When would a trader buy bonds? 93
When would a trader sell bonds? 93

Chapter 6: Options 94

What is the options market? 94
What is an option? 95
How do traders buy and sell options? 96
What does it cost to trade options? 97
How are option prices determined? 97
The valuation of an option contract 98
The Risk/Reward of an option contract 101

Chapter 7: Cryptocurrency 103

What is Cryptocurrency? 103
The different types of cryptocurrencies 109
How was cryptocurrencies created? 113
The Categories of Cryptocurrencies 114
What determines the price of a cryptocurrency? 116
The risk/return of trading cryptocurrencies 118
What is an ICO? 120
What is a Crypto Wallet? 120
How to trade Cryptocurrency 122
Why is cryptocurrency growing so fast? 124

Chapter 8: Strategies and Tips **127**
   When is the best time to trade? 127
   What are the different trading strategies? 128
   How can technical analysis be used in conjunction with fundamental analysis? 131
   What is your Risk Profile? 135
   What is Your Time Frame: 137
Conclusion **139**

Introduction

Welcome to the complete beginner's guide to trading cryptocurrency, forex, stocks, options, futures, and bonds. You will learn everything you need to know about the stock market, trading strategy, and how to become a successful trader. I will teach you everything you need to know. Whether you are a beginner or an expert trader, this guide will be very helpful for you to understand the stock market.

There are many books on the market that will teach you how to become a successful trader. However, most of these books will only teach you how to become a successful trader in the stock market. This book aims to give you a complete understanding of the stock market and how to become a successful trader in all of the markets that exist (including the futures, forex, options, cryptocurrency, stocks, and bonds markets).

It is important to first understand the different markets available in order to understand what you should be focusing on. Each market has a completely different set of rules that you will need to learn in order to become a successful trader. This book will also show you how to use technical analysis, fundamental analysis, and many other different strategies that will allow you to make better trades.

In order to learn how to trade cryptocurrency, forex, stocks, options, futures, and bonds you will need to first understand the mechanisms and strategies that exist in all of these different markets. This book will give you a complete overview of the stock market and each market individually.

Trading cryptocurrency, forex, stocks, options, futures, and bonds can be extremely rewarding if you know the strategies that work in each market.

Let us take a closer look at each of the markets starting with an introduction to the world of trading.

Chapter 1: An Introduction To The World Of Trading

In this chapter I will be giving you a general overview on what trading is and the various forms of trading.

Trading is the process of buying and selling financial assets for a profit. It involves several parties including the buyer, the seller, and the broker who facilitates it all. The seller will set a price that they feel comfortable with, and the buyer will offer less than that price in hopes to close a deal.

There are many different types of trading including:

Stocks - Buying and selling of shares in companies. You can buy an individual share or you can invest in a mutual fund which will pool your money with others and spread your risk.

Options - These are quite complicated and I won't be going into detail on them but essentially it is a contract between two parties where one party has the right to buy or sell an asset at a predetermined price on or before a specific date. You can then profit if the price of the asset goes up or down.

Forex - This is a market where many countries trade their currency to other countries' currency for profit. You can trade currencies themselves, or trade on the movement of currencies against each other (futures).

Futures - A contract that commits to buying/selling an asset at a specific time in the future at a previously agreed upon price. Futures are used to lock in prices for things like commodities like oil, corn, sugar, etc.

Bonds - A type of debt that companies or governments sell in order to raise money. You can buy or sell these bonds depending on if you think the company (or government) will be able to pay you back.

Cryptocurrency - This is a new type of trading based off of blockchain technology. With the price of cryptocurrencies such as Bitcoin, Litecoin, and Ethereum exploding in value lately it is becoming more and more popular.

These are just some of the most common and easiest ones to understand. There are many different types of trading with different risks and rewards. Some of these types of trading can be very risky but also very profitable if you are able to predict the correct movement of the market.

The main forms of trading are stocks, futures, options, forex, bonds, and cryptocurrencies. I will be going into detail on these in the next few chapters. Before we get into more detail, I want to give you an overview of the risks and rewards of trading.

There are many different types of trading and it can be very easy to get confused with all the different terms, risks, and rewards. It is important to understand the basics before you start trading otherwise you will end up losing money.

The different ways of trading

Trading requires strategy and research in order to be successful. There are many different types of trades you can make, and some are riskier than others. The trading strategies that work for one type of trade may not work for another.

There are a few different types of trading, including:

1. Online trading

This form of trading has become extremely popular in recent years. It allows you to trade from your own home without having to hire anyone to help you. When you are trading online, you will be able to make trades 24/7 for some of the most popular assets in the world. Online trading has become so popular because of its convenience and low cost.

For example, if you have some time to kill and are waiting for a friend or family member, you can log in to your trading platform and make a few trades. If you are on vacation, or traveling for work, you can still make trades online. This is one of the biggest advantages of online trading.

Also, there are many online trading platforms that offer you a mobile version of their platform. This enables you to make trades and track your portfolio from anywhere on the move as long as you have an internet connection.

2. Over the phone

You can also make trades over the phone. You can do this with a broker that is either a member of a stock exchange or not. This type of trading is not as popular as it used to be, but there are still some people that use this method of trading.

Most online trading platforms no longer provide this feature to their clients, but there are some platforms that still offer this option.

The retail traders who tend to prefer using a broker over an online trading platform are usually beginners. The reason for this is that they have never traded before, and do not want to spend a lot of time learning how to use an online platform. Sometimes, veteran traders prefer this as this form of placing their orders is the most familiar to them.

3. Over the counter (OTC)

This is a type of trading that is done directly between two entities. These trades are done directly between the two parties without any intermediary. This process is known as over-the-counter trading, or OTC trading for short. It is also known as off-exchange trading when the exchange is a stock exchange and not an alternative form of exchange.

This method of trading developed in order to prevent traders from having to go through the hassle of dealing with multiple brokers and middlemen in order to complete their trades. Money can be transferred directly from one account to another, and this allows traders to avoid having to pay fees on each individual trade they make. This method has become popular with forex traders and some stock market traders because it allows them to make large trades without having to worry about fees associated with each trade they make.

4. Offline trading

This form of trading is also known as over-the-counter trading. This form of trading has actually become less popular in recent years and is usually done by institutional traders.

Instead of the trade being made directly between the two parties, an intermediary is used to complete the trade. This means that one party will not have to send funds directly to another party. The intermediary will receive the funds for one party, and then send those funds on to the other party.

This type of trade is very popular among institutional investors because it allows them to make large trades without having to worry about how they are going to send the money. This type of trading is most popular in the forex market, and is not as common in the stock market.

5. Electronic communications networks (ECNs)

This is one of the least used forms of trading because it has become less popular over the years. This form of trading was created when there was a lack of competition between brokers. ECNs were developed to allow clients to have access to a larger pool of potential buyers and sellers so that they could make trades more easily.

It was believed by some that ECNs would be the future of trading. However, this did not end up being the case. The reason for this is that ECNs do not have any incentives to offer better prices, and they are not as fast at executing trades as online trading platforms are.

Online Trading Platforms

Online trading is by far the most popular and convenient for retail traders such as yourself. In fact, many people are unaware that there are still brokers who operate offline. To maximize your trading experience, it is recommended that you use an online trading platform for the assets that you are planning to trade.

Most of these online platforms provide almost real-time pricing information and charts, enabling you to take advantage of the latest market movements. It is also easy and convenient to place orders online using your laptop or mobile device. In addition, many online trading platforms now allow you to trade forex, stocks, options, futures and even cryptocurrency on the same platform using the same account. It is a lot more convenient for traders who wish to diversify their investments compared to having multiple accounts with multiple brokers.

Brokerage firms and online trading platforms can be broadly categorized into two categories based on their trading platform:

1. ECN Brokers

ECN stands for Electronic Communication Network. These are brokers operate their own servers, and the trades take place directly between the buyer and seller. It is possible to trade directly with other traders on ECN platforms. However, it is often difficult to find a counterparty due to the relatively low liquidity in these platforms. In addition, most ECN brokers charge commission for placing orders, hence making ECN trading costlier compared to traditional offline brokerages.

2. Traditional Trading Platforms

These are online brokerages that use a third-party trading platform such as IB (Interactive Brokers) or Hotspot FX (owned by IG Group). They operate their own servers but use the technology and software provided by third-party companies for trading purposes. These brokerages are more liquid than ECNs and provide traders with more order types such as stop loss and stop limit orders. However, some of them charge higher commissions than others and some of them do not accept US residents as clients. Hence do your homework before you sign up with any of these platforms.

3. Discount Trading Platforms

These are online brokerages that provide clients with the ability to trade online at lower commission rates. The pricing of these discount brokerages are structured differently. Some brokerages offer a flat-fee pricing model where you pay a fixed fee for each trade, while others offer per-share pricing where you pay only for the number of shares that you trade. As you might expect, the former is more cost-effective than the latter.

This type of platform is the most common and the most affordable for retail traders. However, there are some drawbacks associated with discount trading platforms. For example, some of them have a limited number of assets that they can trade and some of them do not accept traders from certain countries as clients. Hence you need to do your research and pick a platform that suits your needs best.

The role of a broker

Brokers are the middlemen that help connect buyers and sellers, allowing them to conduct a trade. Brokers help smooth out the price difference between what people are willing to pay for an asset and what people are willing to sell it for.

It is unlikely that you are able to trade without a broker, unless you are trading in the exchange and clearing the trade yourself.

Brokers are not just limited to a few, they are available in all sizes and shapes. From the large institutional brokers such as Deutsche Bank and Morgan Stanley, which are the big players in the market, to smaller regional brokers that work with retail clients.

The main roles of a broker include:

1. Provide liquidity to the market

The flow of liquidity is vital to the success of the market and ultimately the whole economy. The more liquidity, the better for traders. Liquidity refers to a large amount of buyers and sellers at one time, otherwise known as volume. You want to know you are able to access the markets when you need to trade and that there is enough volume available for you to do so.

2. Provide a platform for investors

Brokers provide traders with tools such as trading platforms, which allow them to access markets quickly and efficiently without having to deal with expensive third-party technology, which would cost traders a lot more money in the long run. The broker will also offer demo accounts where traders can practice trading without risking their own money until they are confident enough in their abilities.

3. Help manage risk and exposure

There is potential for a trader to lose all of their capital through any number of risks such as an adverse market movement, or a lack of control over their emotions during trading sessions. In order for brokers to protect themselves and ensure they get paid, they implement risk management tools designed specifically for each trader's individual needs, including stop loss orders or leverage control tools such as margin calls.

4. Provide a list of trading opportunities

Brokers will provide their clients with many different trading tools and opportunities, including market research and economic calendar events. This way, traders can be sure they are making informed decisions when they execute their trades.

5. Provide professional analysis

If you are not familiar with the markets, research or how the economy moves, brokers can provide you with the knowledge you need to make informed decisions on when or whether to buy or sell assets. They offer technical and fundamental analysis as well as other educational resources that can help you learn how to trade successfully.

With that being said, most of the above roles are now automated in most online trading platforms in the form of e-newsletters and market research.

You really need to consider how you are going to use the broker's services. If you are a beginner, it is unlikely you will be trading on a daily basis as many seasoned traders do, so your main focus should be on building a solid trading strategy that will allow you to trade with confidence and consistency. This will lead to better results in the long run.

Broker Commissions

Commissions are typically charged on a per-trade basis. However, most discount brokerages also offer commission-free trading on some of the assets. It is important to understand that commission-free trading usually comes with some restrictions such as minimum trade sizes, limited asset pairs or currencies, and high trade volumes required to qualify for the same.

In addition, some discount brokerages may also charge additional fees for certain features such as platform usage, withdrawals/deposits, and account inactivity. Hence it is important to read the fine print before you sign up with any of these platforms.

Here are some of the various commission structures that you should be familiar with when selecting a broker:

1. Per-trade Commissions

The most common commission structure that you will find at discount brokerages is the per-trade commissions. Under this structure, the commission is charged for each trade that you place. As a general rule of thumb, the more assets you trade and higher your trade volume, the lower your commissions will be.

For example, some brokers may charge a per-trade commission of $5 for each trade placed on the stock market while others offer a flat rate of $10 for any trade across all asset classes. Some brokerages may also charge tiered rates depending on the size of your trade. Typically, the more volume you trade in a particular asset, the lower the commission that you will be charged.

2. Per-share Commissions

Some discount brokerages may also charge commissions based on the number of shares/contracts traded in a particular stock or contract. These brokerages are often referred to as penny stock brokers since they tend to cater to small investors who are interested in trading penny stocks with minimum investment requirements or smaller lot sizes. For example, some brokerages may charge $0.01 per share for NASDAQ stocks while others may charge higher commissions based on a tiered structure (whereby each tier is associated with a different ticket price).

3. Per-trade + Per-share Commissions

Some discount brokerages may also combine the above two commission structures and impose commissions based on both the number of shares/contracts traded and the price level at which these trades are executed. The rationale behind this type of commission structure is that the commissions will be charged at a lower rate if you execute your trades at a price level with higher liquidity.

For example, if you are trading an ETF but the price at which you execute your trade is $10 higher or lower than the current quote, your broker may charge a commission of $0.01 per share, but if you execute your trades at a price that is near the current quote, the commission will be charged at $0.0025 per share.

4. Commission-free trading

Some discount brokers may also offer commission-free trading on select asset classes as an incentive for traders to open an account with them. Typically, these brokerages will charge additional fees for certain features such as platform usage, withdrawals/deposits, and account inactivity. Hence it is important to read the fine print before you sign up with any of these platforms.

5. Volume-based discounts

Some brokerages may also try to incentivize their customers by charging a lower commission rate if they meet certain trade volume requirements. For example, a discount brokerage may charge a per-trade commission of $5 for NASDAQ stocks but waive the same if the individual trades at least 500 shares within a given year.

6. Other

Some discount brokerages may also charge additional fees for certain features such as platform usage, withdrawals/deposits, and account inactivity. Hence it is important to read the fine print before you sign up with any of these platforms.

Commissions can be paid upfront (when you place your order) or deferred (when you close your trade).

In the former case, the brokerage will charge you upfront for all the commissions that you are likely to incur over the lifetime of your trade. For example, if you place a long-term buy order on Amazon stock and it takes several months for this trade to be filled, your broker may charge a commission every single time you place an order in addition to any other fees that may be charged based on your trading activity.

In the latter case, commissions will be charged only when you close your trade. For example, if you place a long-term buy order on

Amazon stock and it takes several months for this trade to be filled, your broker will charge you a single commission when the trade is closed.

If commissions are charged upfront, it is important that you understand each of the fees that may be charged over the lifetime of your trade. If commissions are deferred, you should just make sure that your broker does not charge exorbitant fees upon trade closure.

Broker Fees

Besides commissions, most discount brokerages also charge additional fees for certain features such as platform usage, withdrawals/deposits, and account inactivity. Hence it is important to read the fine print before you sign up with any of these platforms. Here are some of the various fees that you should be familiar with when selecting a broker:

1. Platform fees

Some brokerages may also charge additional fees for using their platform to place trades. Typically, these charges will apply on a per-trade basis and may range from $0.50 to $5 per trade depending on the asset class and the specific brokerage. Hence, it is important to make sure that you are not overpaying for trading commissions if you use your discount brokerage's platform to place trades.

2. Withdrawal/deposit fees

Some brokerages may also charge additional fees for performing withdrawals or deposits into or from your account. Hence it is important that you understand the fee structures associated with various activities before opening an account with any of these platforms. For example, some brokerages may charge a flat fee of $20 for withdrawals while others may charge a percentage-based fee (such as 1% of the amount withdrawn). Similarly, some platforms may also levy additional fees for transferring funds from one account to another within the same brokerage (such as moving funds from your trading account to your cash account). While others don't charge anything at all! Hence it is important that you verify these details before you sign up with any of these brokerages.

3. Account inactivity fees

Some brokerages may also charge additional fees for account inactivity, such as quarterly or annual fees that are charged simply because you have not conducted any transactions on your account during the past year or so. However, most discount brokerage platforms do not charge any such fees and hence you should make sure that you are not overpaying for an account that is not being used!

4. Paper statement fee

Some brokerages may also charge additional fees for printing and mailing statements to customers who would like to receive hard copies of their account statements in the mail. Hence it is important to understand whether such a fee applies before you open an account with any of these platforms.

5. Minimum deposit/balance requirements

Some discount brokerages may also require minimum initial deposits or minimum balance requirements before you can begin trading on the platform. Hence it is important that you understand and verify these requirements before opening an account with any of these platforms, and avoid overpaying by choosing a platform that does not have such restrictions on your account!

6. Additional fees for special services

Some brokerages may also charge additional fees for certain special services, such as expedited wire transfers or margin calls. Hence it is important that you verify the availability of such services and the associated fees before you choose a discount brokerage platform!

Operational Hours of Trading Markets

Certain asset types can only be traded during certain times of the day, while others can be traded 24 hours a day, 7 days a week. Before you start trading, you will need to be aware of when the markets are open and closed. Each market has a different time schedule on when they open and close. Some online trading platforms will still allow you to place your orders even when the markets are closed. However, you will not be able to see your trades on your account until the trading market is open.

The following is a list of various markets and their general operational hours:

Forex Markets:

The forex market is the most liquid market in the world. The average trade is completed in just a few seconds. This intraday trading market is open 24 hours a day, 5 days a week. Different currency pairs have different operational hours. You will have to check with your broker to see when the market is open and closed.

For example, the EUR/USD is the most popular currency pair. The operational hours for this pair is 6pm GMT Sunday - 5pm GMT Friday. This means that a trade can be placed at 6pm GMT on Sunday and will be executed at 5pm GMT on Friday. If you place a trade outside of these hours, it will not be executed until the next session opens.

Stock Markets:

Different stock markets from around the world are open 24 hours a day, 5 days a week. However, some markets may be closed on certain holidays. You should check with your broker to see what the operational hours are for each market that you wish to trade.

For example, the New York Stock Exchange (NYSE) is open from 9:30am-4:00pm Eastern Time Monday through Friday. The NASDAQ Stock Market is open from 4:00pm - 8:59pm Eastern Time Monday through Friday.

Bond Markets:

Generally, the bond market opens from 8:00am-3:00pm Eastern Time Monday through Friday. Each bond market will have their own operational hours and holidays. There are some bond markets that are open 24 hours a day, 7 days a week.

If you will be trading bonds, you will need to check with your broker to find out their operational hours.

Options Markets:

Options markets can be traded 24 hours a day, but each exchange may have their own operational hours. You will need to check with your broker to find out what the operational hours are for each of the markets that you wish to trade.

For example, the Chicago Board Options Exchange (CBOE) is open from 8:30am-3:15pm Eastern Time Monday through Friday. The International Securities Exchange (ISE) is open from 6:00pm - 5:00am Eastern Time Monday through Friday.

Futures Markets:

Each futures market has their own operational hours and holidays. There are some futures markets that are open 24 hours a day, 7 days a week. If you plan on trading futures, you will need to check with your broker for their operational hours and holidays.

For example, the Chicago Mercantile Exchange (CME) is open from 6:00am-4:00pm Central Time Monday through Friday. The New York Mercantile Exchange (NYMEX) is open from 8:00am-3:55pm Eastern Time Monday through Friday.

Cryptocurrency Markets:

All cryptocurrency markets are opened 24 hours a day, 7 days a week. There are no holidays in the cryptocurrency markets.

To summarize, all trading markets have different operational hours when they open and close. Before you start trading, you will need to check with your broker to see what the operational hours are for each market that you wish to trade.

Special holidays to note:

For the trading markets with fixed hours, there are some special holidays that you may want to note. These holidays may create market volatility and will increase trading volume especially for forex and stock markets.

The following are a list of holidays that you may want to take note of:

1. New Year's Day

Most financial markets will be closed on this day. If they are open, there will usually be minimal trading volume. This day is a holiday in all countries that trade with the United States. It is also a holiday for most European countries and Australia.

2. Martin Luther King Day

This day is a holiday in the United States, but is not a paid holiday for stock markets. Stock markets will be open on this day. There will be low volume trading on this day and there may be some volatility. This day is also a holiday for Canada and Mexico.

3. Good Friday

This is a voluntary holiday that banks in Ireland, the United Kingdom and some other European countries observe. Most financial markets are closed on this day with the exception of the London Stock Exchange which has normal hours of operation. This day is not considered a public or bank holiday in all countries that trade with the United States. This is a religious holiday observed by Christians around the world to remember Jesus Christ's crucifixion and death at Calvary before His resurrection three days later on Easter Sunday.

4. Easter Sunday/Easter Monday

This is a public holiday for most European countries, Australia and New Zealand. The London Stock Exchange may have normal hours of operation on this day, depending upon what country you are located in when you are trading from (for example if you are located in London then the LSE will have normal hours). If you are located outside the LSE's operational hours, then there will be little to no trading on this day.

5. Independence Day (July 4th)

This is not considered a public or bank holiday for any country that trades with the United States. It is a federal holiday in the United States and stock markets will be open on this day with low volume trading expected. This day will have high volumes of trading for forex and futures markets because it coincides with monthly expiry dates which may create volatility in these markets.

The benefits of trading

Now that we have covered the fundamentals of how trading markets work and how to use and trade them, let's take a look at the benefits of becoming a retail trader. There are numerous benefits to be found in trading markets, and it is the reason that there are so many players in the market.

Let's take a look at how trading markets can be so beneficial to us as investors and traders.

1. Trading is very flexible:

The great benefit to trading is that it is extremely flexible to the person who wants to trade. Most markets are open 24 hours a day, 5 days a week. There are no restrictions on when you can enter or exit a trade, unlike in a job or some business.

If you are on vacation, or just do not want to be at your computer at a certain time, you can put your trades on "hold" and come back when you have time.

Furthermore, you get to decide on what you want to trade, and how you want to trade it. You can trade on your own terms.

2. Trading can be lucrative:

This is one of the best things about trading, that it can be very profitable. The key is to learn as much as you can about the markets you want to trade in and take advantage of that knowledge. There is no limit to how much you can make, although there is a limit to how much you can lose.

If you have a good knowledge of the markets and trade them wisely, you can make a lot of money while having fun in the process.

In the world of trading, it's always a good idea to keep a cool head and not get caught up in the excitement of trading. Remember, trading can be very risky if you are not careful and make bad decisions. If you are winning in your trades, you can be sure that someone else is losing in their trades.

Remember that even professional institutional traders get around a 50% hit rate in their trades. These are the top traders that make a lot of money doing what they do.

The reality is that you will lose more trades than you win, but the key to trading success is to minimize your losses by cutting your losses and letting your profits run, and not giving back those profits.

3. You are able to use leverage

Unlike in a job or a small business, you can use leverage when you trade. Leverage is the ability to make larger trades with smaller capital amounts. This is a way to magnify your gains and losses by trading with more money than you have in your account.

For example, if you have $5,000 in your trading account, but you want to be able to trade with $10,000, you can use leverage to do so. Most online trading platforms will have a margin trading service, whereby you can trade with up to 100x leverage, meaning you can control $100,000 in a $5,000 account.

However, this is also a very risky proposition. If you lose money, the trading platform will still have to pay the $100,000 amount. As such, if you are using leverage, it is very important that you set a stop-loss order so that if a trade goes against you and hits your stop-loss point, the trade is closed out immediately to protect your account.

Using this tool, you can make more money or lose more money fast, depending on how you use it.

4. Trading is a game:

This is one of the most exciting things about trading. Trading is a game, and it's fun to play.

The fact is, it's a game that you are playing with other traders and the market. Some people say that trading can be addicting and fun, which is why they keep playing. There is something about trading that makes it fun to engage in. It's like playing blackjack or craps in a casino, but there is more skill involved in trading than those games.

It's very exciting to be able to make money while having fun playing a game online. It's even better because you can make money at your own pace and on your own schedule.

5. Trading is social:

Trading has become very social these days due to the advent of online communication tools such as Skype, Slack, Telegram, Discord etc. There are many people who use these tools to trade together in real-time and share ideas and experiences. This social aspect of trading takes some of the stress out of trading and makes the process more enjoyable for many traders.

While trading can be extremely profitable if done correctly, it also comes with great risk just like any other investment strategy or activity out there. It's important that you educate yourself as much as possible before you start trading to minimize the risks involved.

Don't think that only small-time retail traders are in social discussion groups and sharing information about their trades - large institutional and professional traders do so on their sophisticated Bloomberg terminals.

6. Low capital requirements:

Unlike starting a business, you don't need a lot of capital to start trading. You can start trading with as little as $50 in the stock market or forex. If you want to start trading options, you should have at least $500 in your account, but it could be less depending on how much leverage you decide to use.

7. Trading is not illegal:

In some countries, you might be able to get into trouble with the law if you choose to trade online and make money from it because it's viewed as gambling or a form of illegal activity. However, in most countries including the US and Europe, trading is legal and not considered a form of gambling unlike in other parts of the world such as Asia and Africa. This makes it easier for traders from other countries to enter the online trading community because they are not breaking any laws by engaging in online trading.

The disadvantage of trading

I would argue that there are almost no disadvantages to trading, unless you do not know how to do it. Your mindset and control over your emotions are the key factors to successful trading. Inexperienced retail investors will see and experience the majority of the disadvantages associated with trading due to their lack of understanding and unpreparedness.

Trading is a very risky activity that requires you to have the right knowledge and experience, otherwise you will lose your money. You have to be willing to take risks, because that's what trading is all about. If you are not able to handle the emotions that come from being in a riskier situation, then I would advise you not to trade until you are ready.

Here are some of the downsides to trading that inexperienced investors may experience:

1. Losing money

Yes, the number one disadvantage is losing money. If you do not understand how to trade and lose your money, you will lose a lot of it. Trading is a high-risk activity that requires you to be in control of your emotions and have the right knowledge. If you are unable to do either of them, then trading is not the right activity for you.

This is the number one reason why most beginner retail traders exit the market altogether and why most people do not want to even get started. Losing money is a very big deal and it happens more than you might think.

The truth is that everyone is afraid and hates losing money. However, as a trader you have to accept that it is the cost of doing business and that you will lose money. The only thing you can do is to minimize your losses and learn from your mistakes.

It will not be possible not to lose money when you are trading in the markets. This is the reality and you have to accept it. It will happen even if you are a professional trader, so do not think that you will be the exception. If you want to be successful in the markets, then you have to accept that losing money is a part of trading.

2. Being nervous or stressed out all of the time

Being in control of one's emotions is one of the most important factors when it comes to trading successfully. If you cannot control your emotions, then you will not be successful in the markets. This is one of the biggest reasons why a lot of traders do not succeed because they let their emotions get the better of them.

In order to be successful as a trader, you have to have a high tolerance for risk and be in control of your emotions. The markets can get pretty stressful and nerve-wracking at times, so if you are not able to handle that effectively, then you will lose money.

3. Getting greedy

This is another major mistake that most retail traders make and it leads them to losing money. When you enter the market with a trade, it is important that you have a well-defined exit plan in place before entering the trade. If you do not have an exit plan in place before entering your trade, then this will lead to unnecessary losses along with some emotional frustration as well.

If you are able to identify when your trades are going against you, then it is much easier for you to get out at an earlier stage and minimize your losses before they grow into something bigger than what they started off as. It is important that every trader has an exit plan in place before entering a trade to avoid unnecessary losses.

4. Getting too emotional

In most cases, the biggest problem that novice traders face is getting too emotional. This is one of the reasons why people fail to be successful in the markets and it's due to their inability to be in control of their emotions. If you let your emotions get the better of you, then you will lose a lot of money.

It is important that you do not let your emotions get the better of you and that you keep a calm and rational mind at all times. It is hard to do, but it is possible if you are willing to put in the time and effort. Once again, this comes down to experience and how much time you spend in front of your charts and trading platform.

5. Getting Scammed

There are a lot of scammers in the financial markets and a lot of shady activity. It is very easy to get scammed in the markets and it can happen to any trader, even those who are more experienced. Scammers are always looking for new ways to trick people and make money off of them, so be careful out there and do not trust anyone blindly.

6. Not having any income

If you are not able to trade successfully, then you will not have any income or at least not enough income to offset your expenses. This is why it is important that you practice trading on a demo account before entering real money into the markets. If you are not able to trade effectively with fake money, then you will not be able to do it with real money either.

Most often, being a retail trader will involve doing it part time while you have a job or other sources of income. This is because it is very difficult to generate consistent profits in the markets and you will not be able to quit your job if you do not have consistent success.

Retail trading is all about making consistent profits and increasing your capital with each trade. If you are not able to make consistent profits, then you will never be able to trade successfully full time and generate an income from it.

7. Losing confidence

This is one of the biggest reasons why people fail as traders because they lose confidence in themselves and their ability to trade successfully. Losing confidence can make a person give up, so it is important that you don't lose confidence in yourself or your abilities if things don't go exactly as planned. It is also important that you take some time off from the markets in order to allow yourself some time to rest and recharge before getting back into the game again.

8. Falling into debt

In particular, leveraged retail traders who make use of margin accounts that are provided by online trading platforms form the biggest group of traders that are prone to falling into debt. These traders have to be extra careful when trading because of the high level of risks associated with margin trading. You should avoid margin trading as much as possible if you are a beginner.

There are some online trading platforms that make trading on a margin account enticing by offering a high margin ratio of up to 100X of your initial deposit. This means that if you are trading with a $100 dollar margin account, your trade size can be as high as $10,000 dollars.

This type of investment strategy tends to attract beginner traders as well as the experienced ones because it offers a high profit potential. However, it comes with a high risk.

A beginner trader who makes use of a margin account can easily fall into the debt trap. This is because of the higher profits that can be realized. However, you should be cautious because the losses you incur due to margin trading can also be massive.

A beginner trader should not trade on a margin account with more than 50% of the initial deposit. This means that you should never trade with more than half of your initial deposit in your trading account.

9. Trading can be addictive

Trading can be addictive. A lot of people get addicted to trading because they enjoy the thrill that is associated with it. Many retail traders only know how to speculate and make profits on a short-term basis.

This kind of trading is usually referred to as day trading. Day traders tend to sit in front of their computer screens all day long watching the price action of a particular stock. They usually buy and sell in very small increments within a few minutes.

The emotions of speculating in the trading markets are comparable to that of gambling, as both activities provide the same excitement and thrill, which can lead to addiction and potentially more problems.

It is important to note that trading can be an addiction. Being addicted to trading can lead you to lose more money than you make. It is important to be aware of this fact so that you will not fall into the same trap.

Technical analysis

Technical analysis is a method of trading that can be used for any financial market. It involves the use of various indicators and charts which help traders make decisions regarding when and where to buy or sell an asset.

Over the years, it has gained popularity among traders who are always looking for the best way to profit from trading.

The most important aspect of technical analysis is to always use a strategy that works well in all conditions.

The reason why technical analysis works well is that it is based primarily on the historical data.

For traders who are just starting out, it is recommended that they should stick to the basics.

The beginner traders should start with simple strategies that include trend analysis, support and resistance, candlestick patterns and moving averages.

Technical analysis can be used for any asset class including equities, commodities, forex and cryptocurrencies. However, most of the time it is mostly used for stocks trading since they have more historical data available.

One of the best ways to learn about technical analysis is by observing the price action of a stock or commodity. The best way to learn about it is by reading books or watching YouTube videos by renowned traders who explain their strategy in detail. This approach will help you get a better understanding of how technical analysis works and how you can make use of it in your trading strategy.

Given that most online trading platforms provide you the necessary and accurate historical information regarding the price action of a particular asset, it is recommended that you start analyzing the charts of a particular asset to get a better understanding of technical analysis.

The most important aspect of technical analysis is that it helps traders understand how the other traders are trading an asset. Therefore, it is important to understand that the price of an asset is not only determined by the fundamental factors but also by how other traders are trading it.

Here are the basic terminologies that are used in technical analysis:

1. Candlestick chart

A candlestick chart is one of the most important elements of a technical analysis. It basically shows the high, low and close prices of a particular asset during a certain period.

The color of the candle indicates the price action. Green or white candles indicate that the price is rising while red or black candles indicate that the price is falling. The wicks on both ends represent the top and bottom prices during that period. The red candlesticks indicate that more sellers are coming in compared to buyers, thereby pushing down the price while green candles indicate that more buyers are coming in compared to sellers, thereby pushing up the price.

Candlesticks show you whether the price is trending up or down and they also show you if it is overbought or oversold at any given moment in time. This is one of the most important aspects of technical analysis since it gives you a better understanding of how the other traders are trading the stock at any given moment in time.

2. Support and resistance

Every chart has an imaginary line which shows you the highest and lowest price during a certain period. This imaginary line is known as the support or resistance line.

3. Moving average convergence divergence (MACD)

MACD is basically a momentum indicator that helps traders determine whether a stock is overbought or oversold at any given moment in time. It can be used for any asset class including equities, commodities, forex and cryptocurrencies.

The MACD indicator is one of the most important indicators for traders who are looking to make money from short-term trading. However, it does not really work well for longer term trading since it tends to become less effective once the price action starts moving sideways. Therefore, it is recommended that you use this indicator for short-term trading only. In fact, it should be used along with other indicators so that they complement each other to give you an edge over other traders on the market. The best way to use this indicator would be to combine it with Bollinger Bands or Simple Moving Average (SMA) to determine the points at which you'll enter or exit a trade.

4. RSI

Another important indicator that works well with MACD is the Relative Strength Index (RSI). It works by measuring the speed and change of prices. The RSI can be used for any asset class including equities, commodities, forex and cryptocurrencies.

5. Candlestick chart patterns

Candlestick chart patterns are a very important indicator of a technical analysis since it helps traders determine how other traders are trading an asset at any given moment in time. This is one of the most important aspects of technical analysis since it helps you understand how other traders are trading an asset if you know what candlestick pattern they have formed to indicate their buy or sell orders. In fact, it doesn't matter if a particular candlestick pattern has already formed on your charts as long as you have enough information about it and know when and where to buy or sell based on that pattern. There are many different types of candlesticks patterns such as engulfing candle, spinning top, doji candle and hammer candle etc.. Each one of them indicates something different based on their shape and color.

6. Volume indicator

Volume indicator basically shows how many stocks or commodities have traded in a particular period of time. It is one of the most important aspects of technical analysis since it helps traders determine the volume and activity of a stock or commodity at any given moment in time. This is one of the most important aspects for traders who are looking to trade from a longer term perspective. Therefore, it is recommended that traders use this indicator in combination with other indicators so that they can gain an edge on the market.

Fundamental analysis

Fundamental analysis on the other hand is a method of analyzing a security that has some intrinsic value based on the performance of an underlying company, economic sector, or group of companies.

In the case of cryptocurrencies, most investors and traders will use fundamental analysis to decide which cryptocurrencies to buy. For example, you might decide to invest in a cryptocurrency because it's price is currently low and you believe that the team is going to announce some good news in the future. You might also be able to predict the price of a cryptocurrency based on how well the underlying technology is performing.

One of the most common ways to perform fundamental analysis on cryptocurrencies is to look at the level of adoption. For example, if a cryptocurrency has a large number of merchants that accept it as a form of payment, there will be more demand for the cryptocurrency, and this should push up the price.

Another example would be if you were able to predict that a new technology was going to be developed soon that would make use of the underlying cryptocurrency technology. This could also push up the price in anticipation of this event happening in the future.

Let's take a look at the terminologies used in fundamental analysis.

1. Price-to-Earnings Ratio

The Price-to-Earnings Ratio (P/E) is the ratio of the price of a company's stock to its earnings per share, and it is a measure of the value of a company's stock. The P/E ratio is usually calculated by dividing the price of a stock by its earnings per share.

For example, if a stock has an earnings per share of $1, but it is trading at $3 then the P/E ratio would be 3. If the earnings per share were $10 and the price was still $3 then the P/E ratio would be 10.

You might also hear traders talk about trailing and forward P/E ratios. The trailing P/E ratio considers only one year's worth of earnings in relation to a stock's current price, whereas forward P/E ratios consider next year's estimated earnings in relation to today's price. For example, if a stock has had an annual growth rate of 10% over the last five years, you could calculate its trailing five-year average as (5 years x 10%) + (5 years x 2%) = 15%. You could then divide this figure by today's price to get an idea of whether or not you should buy this security.

2. Price-to-Book Ratio

The Price-to-Book Ratio (P/B) is a popular ratio among fundamental analysts who value the intrinsic value of a stock. The P/B ratio is the price of a stock relative to its book value.

Book Value is equal to the total assets of a company, minus intangible assets and liabilities, divided by the number of shares outstanding. The book value per share gives an investor an idea of how much they are paying for each dollar worth of assets in a company. If you compare two companies with similar earnings and growth rates, but one company has a lower P/B ratio than the other, it could be an indication that you should buy the second company since it's shares are cheaper than the other company's shares.

3. Sales Growth Rate

Sales growth rate is a measurement of how fast a company's sales are growing over time. It is calculated by dividing year-over-year sales by last year's sales and multiplying it by 100%. It is important to look for companies that have consistent positive sales growth rates over 10 years or more because these are companies that have proven themselves to be able to sell their products and services during different economic cycles. This is sometimes referred to as the "compound annual growth rate".

4. Earnings Per Share

Earnings Per Share (EPS) is the amount of profit a company makes on each share of its stock. It is calculated by dividing the company's net income by the number of outstanding shares and multiplying it by 100%. If you are comparing two companies with similar sales growth rates but one has a higher EPS than the other, then it could be an indication that you should buy the second company since its earnings are growing faster than the other company.

5. Dividend Payout Ratio

A dividend payout ratio tells you how much of a company's earnings have been paid to investors as dividends. For example, if a company pays out 50% of its profits in dividends then this means that 50% of all profits have been returned to shareholders via dividends. The ratio can also be calculated using the current stock price rather than the stock's price during previous years and this is sometimes referred to as "trailing dividend payout ratio".

Here are some unique fundamental analysis terminologies for cryptocurrency investors and traders.

1. Transaction Count

Transactions are counted whenever a cryptocurrency is moved from one wallet to another. In order for a cryptocurrency to be able to be used for anything, it needs a large number of transactions coming in and out of its network.

For example, Bitcoin has the largest number of transactions per day than any other cryptocurrency, and this is one of the reasons why it is widely accepted as a form of payment by merchants.

2. TPS

Transactions Per Second (TPS) is a measurement of how many transactions can be processed by the blockchain network in one second. When you compare the TPS of different cryptocurrencies you can get an idea if they are able to handle large numbers of transactions quickly. If you see that one cryptocurrency has a high number of transactions but another cryptocurrency has a much higher TPS this might give you an indication that the second cryptocurrency will probably become more widely adopted in the future since it can handle more users at once without slowing down its network.

3. Mining Difficulty Rate

The Mining Difficulty Rate (MDR) is an indicator that tells us how hard it is to mine new coins on any given blockchain network. If the MDR increases then it becomes harder to mine coins and this could mean that the price is going to drop.

The MDR is measured in two ways: the 'Hashrate' and the 'Total Difficulty'. Hashrate is the amount of mining power that a blockchain network has. The total difficulty on the other hand is a measurement of how much computation work has been done by all of the miners in order to find new blocks.

4. SegWit & SegWit2x

SegWit, or Segregated Witness, is a change in how transactions are stored and verified on any given blockchain network. You will see this terminology mainly associated with Bitcoin and its forks (Bitcoin Cash, Bitcoin Gold etc), but it could also be relevant for other cryptocurrencies that use similar technology to Bitcoin such as Litecoin and Dash. If you see this term being mentioned in cryptocurrency discussion groups on Reddit or Discord, it might be an indicator to you that the price of these cryptocurrencies could be going up soon since they can process more transactions at once.

5. Hard Fork & Softfork

A blockchain hard fork happens when there is a change to the underlying protocol of a cryptocurrency that requires all miners and nodes running on that blockchain network to update their software before they can continue to use the network. Sometimes this occurs when the blockchain needs to be upgraded to add new features or fix a bug that has been discovered. If you see a lot of discussion about hardforks on Reddit or Discord, it could be an indicator that the price of a cryptocurrency is going up. This is because there might be some positive news coming in the future, and investors want to buy their coins while they are still cheap before this happens

A blockchain soft fork on the other hand is just a change in how a cryptocurrency works that doesn't require all of its users to update their software before they can continue using it. This means that no matter what version of software you are using, you will still be able to send and receive transactions on the network as usual.

If you see some comment in discussion groups on Reddit or Discord asking which version of software someone should use, this could indicate something positive for that cryptocurrency since there might be some upcoming changes that will make it more useful. For example, if two different softforks were being discussed on Reddit then it might indicate that one fork was going to allow for faster transactions while another fork was going to allow for more privacy so investors are trying to decide which one to use.

6. Pump & Dump

Pump and Dump groups are what happens when a group of people decide to buy a cryptocurrency for the purpose of causing price increase and then cashing out quickly before the price drops. In order to make money from pump and dump groups, you need to be able to move your money in and out of cryptocurrencies quickly. This is why a lot of pump and dump groups will only accept cryptocurrencies like Bitcoin or Litecoin so that they don't have to wait for bank transfers or wire payments to clear before they make their trades. The most successful pump and dump scams are usually run by people who already hold a large number of coins in the cryptocurrency that they are trying to manipulate.

For example, if someone already had 100 coins in Dogecoin, then it would be easy for them to get together with other investors who also have 100 Dogecoins, buy 1000 more from an exchange, then start talking about how good Dogecoin is on Reddit or Discord so that everyone starts buying it up until the price has gone up so much that they can sell all their new coins for a large profit. After this has happened, they might start selling their old coins as well since there is a risk that the price could come crashing down if everyone decides to sell at once.

7. Bull Bear

Bulls and Bears are investors who think that the price of a cryptocurrency is going to go up or down in the future. If you see a lot of people talking about how the market is going to be bullish or bearish, this could indicate that a lot of people are trying to predict what the price is going to do next, and this could be an indicator for you as well. For example, if you see a lot of comments about how 'bullish' the markets are, it might mean that a lot of people are expecting the price to go up so it would be a good time for you to buy your coins before they become more expensive. On the other hand, if you see comments from people saying that they think 'bearish' then it might mean that they believe the price will drop soon and it would be better for you to wait until after this happens before you invest in any cryptocurrencies.

Here are some unique fundamental analysis terminologies for bond investors and traders.

1. CPI

The Consumer Price Index (CPI) is a measurement of how much prices are going up or down in the economy. It can be used as an indicator for the future direction of interest rates and it is usually reported monthly by the government. If you see a large increase in the CPI, this could indicate that the Federal Reserve will raise interest rates soon to help slow down inflation. However, if you see a decrease in the CPI, this could mean that a rate cut will happen instead since there is not as much inflation risk.

2. Yield

The yield of a bond is the annual interest payment that you will receive on the bond. It is usually expressed as a percentage of the face value of the bond. For example, if you buy a $1,000 bond and receive an 8% yield, you will receive $80 in interest payments per year. If the yield increases, this could indicate that the bond is becoming more attractive to investors and this could push up the price. If it decreases, it could be a sign that people are losing confidence in the underlying security and that it might drop in price.

3. Duration

Duration is used to calculate one specific thing: how much a bond's price will change if interest rates change by 1%. For example, if you know that your bond has a duration of 5 years and interest rates drop by 1%, you can expect half of your capital to disappear since your investment will not earn enough interest payments to compensate for this loss (you should have sold it before this happened). If the duration increases for a security this usually means that there's an expectation for higher rates in the future which should push up its price. However, if it decreases then it could mean that there's an expectation for lower rates in the future which should push down its price.

4. Price / Yield Correlation

The price / yield correlation of a bond is a measure of how much the bond's price changes when there is a change in its yield. For example, if the price of a bond moves in the same direction as its yield, this means that bonds with similar characteristics will have similar prices. If their prices move in opposite directions then they will be considered to be negatively correlated and this could mean that investors are losing confidence in both of them.

5. Yield Curve

The yield curve is an interest rate curve that shows all of the available interest rates for maturities ranging from 3 month to 30 years on government bonds and other securities. If you know where you want to invest your money and you know what maturity you are looking for, you can use it to figure out what interest rates are available at these maturities and compare them to each other. It can also be used as an indicator for future economic activity since it shows how people think things will look like in the future relative to today (if they expect lower rates they won't want to invest their money at higher rates for a long time and this will push down the yield curve, if they expect higher rates they will want to invest at higher rates for a long time which will push up the yield curve).

Here are some unique fundamental analysis terminologies that are used by traders and investors in the forex markets.

1. Employment Rate

The employment rate is a measure of how many people are working in a country and it is usually expressed as a percentage of the total population. A high employment rate is usually considered to be a good thing since it means that more people are earning income and this can help push up the price of the currency. However, if the employment rate is dropping rapidly, this could indicate that there is going to be a recession which could cause investors to lose confidence in the currency and this could cause its price to drop.

2. Inflation Rate

Inflation is usually considered to be a bad thing for currencies since it means that money will be losing value over time and this can hurt economic growth. Inflation rates are usually calculated by comparing the cost of goods between two different years (say 2015 vs 2016) and reporting what percent change there was in costs between these two years (for example, if apple costs $1 in 2015 but $1.10 in 2016 then inflation would be 10% since you have to pay

10 cents more for apples than you did one year ago). The higher the inflation rate, the more likely investors will want to invest their money in other assets with higher returns (like stocks) instead so they can protect the purchasing power of their money.

3. Export / Import Ratio

The export / import ratio shows what percent of a country's exports are sold to another country and what percent are sold to third party countries. This is an important indicator because it can indicate to investors how dependent the country's economy is on other countries and how much it relies on the rest of the world for growth. If exports have a high share of imports then this means that the country is highly dependent on trade and if it has a low share this means that it is not as dependent on trade (this could be due to its own domestic market being large enough to support exports).

This could indicate that the currency will be more stable since there is less risk of trade wars impacting its economy and causing its currency value to drop. In some cases, trade wars can actually benefit certain currencies since they make them more competitive in overseas markets (this is called an export-led recovery). However, if a country has a very high export / import ratio, this can also indicate that it does not produce many goods itself which could make it vulnerable in case there are supply shortages (this would be bad for its currency since prices would have to rise).

Here are some fundamental analysis terminologies that are used by traders and investors in the futures and options markets.

1. Gross Domestic Product

The Gross Domestic Product (GDP) is the total value of all final goods and services produced by a country in a given period (usually a year). It is one of the most commonly used indicators to measure economic growth. If you want to know how well the economy is doing you can compare this measurement with previous years to see how it changed.

2. Consumer Price Index

This is a measurement of the average price of goods and services purchased by individuals. If this number is increasing it means that it's getting more expensive to live in that country. As a result, the value of the currency will decrease because people will buy less of it.

3. Inflation Rate

This is the percentage rate at which the price of goods and services in an economy increase over a certain period of time. It's calculated by dividing the Consumer Price Index by 100 and multiplying it by the period you want to look at (usually a year).

4. Environmental Factors

There are a number of factors that can affect the performance of an economy. Environmental factors like natural disasters such as floods, hurricanes and earthquakes can have a huge impact on the economy and on the price of the country's currency.

5. Consumer Activity and sentiment

The activity of consumers in an economy can have a huge impact on the currency and it's price. If for example, the consumer confidence is low, people will be less likely to spend and they will keep their money in savings. For futures and options, this can lead to an increase in the demand for safe haven assets such as gold.

6. Inflationary pressures

This is the rate at which inflation increases over time. It's usually calculated by dividing the change in the consumer price index by the previous year and multiplying it by 100 (this gives you a percentage).

7. Federal Funds Rate

This is one of the most important interest rates in any economy, especially for forex traders. When the Federal Funds Rate is increased the value of the currency will drop because investors will sell their currency to buy dollars in order to benefit from the higher interest rates.

8. The Business Cycle

The business cycle is a series of alternating periods of economic expansion and contraction. This cycle is usually represented by a line graph that shows inflation, GDP, unemployment rates and other economic measures over time. Sometimes this cycle can last for several years (like it did in 2008 and 2009), but it can also be very short (a few months or even weeks). Understanding the business cycle can help you predict what will happen next.

Types of Trade Orders

Many online trading platforms offer retail traders the ability to place a trade by clicking on a button for a particular type of trade order. However, more sophisticated retail traders will want to automate their trades by making use of the various types of trade orders that are offered. In this section, we will be looking at the various types of trade orders that you can utilize to automate your trades.

These trade orders are available on most online trading platforms and for most asset classes, including currencies, forex, stocks, commodities, and even digital assets like cryptocurrencies. There are two main types of trade orders: market orders and limit orders.

1. Market Orders

A market order is an order to buy or sell a security at the current market price. When you enter a market order, your trade will be instantly filled and you will be charged the current price of the asset. When a trader wants to trade an asset quickly without worrying about the price, they usually place a market order. A market order is also known as an "at-the-market" (ATM) order.

Market orders are best suited for those who are looking to execute trades immediately and do not care about the price at which they are filled. Market orders can be placed by choosing a specific number of shares or contracts from the available choices on your trading platform, by selecting a percentage of your total holdings in an asset, or by inputting a specific amount in your account's currency.

For example, say you enter a buy market order with the price of EUR/USD at 1.1350, this means that you are looking to buy the EUR currency pair at the current market price. The order will be filled at any price between 1.1349 and 1.1351. So, if the EUR/USD rate drops to 1.1345 after you place your trade, your trade will be filled at this price. If it goes up to 1.1355, then your trade will be filled at this price as well.

Market orders are best suited for traders who want to make a quick trade and do not care about the exact price that they are getting in or out of a market. However, market orders are not recommended for traders who are new to trading because placing a market order is very different from traditional investment methods.

In the stock markets, when you place a market order you are effectively telling your broker to "buy me whatever stocks are available at the current price." However, in the forex markets, the current price includes all of the bid and ask prices for an asset.

A market order in this case means that your trade will be filled at a price that is worse than what a limit order may have filled you at. When making use of market orders, traders should be aware of their entry and exit prices to ensure that they are not getting in or out of a market at a less than favorable price.

2. Limit Orders

A limit order is an order to buy or sell a security at a specific price or better. When you place a limit order, you are telling your broker to "buy me this asset at the price mentioned in my trade order or better." Therefore, if the current price of the asset is below your desired purchase price, then you will not get filled on your trade. If the current price of the asset is above your desired purchase price, then you will get filled but you will not get filled at your preferred entry point.

Limit orders are best suited for those who want to enter a market, but only at a specific price point. Limit orders can be placed using sliders on most online trading platforms. Some platforms may also have an order form that allows traders to input specific amounts in their account's currency and choose their desired entry and exit prices.

For example, say that you are looking to buy EUR/USD at 1.1300 and an EUR/USD rate of 1.1303 is available on your trading platform. You place a limit order with this price but the EUR/USD rate falls to 1.1298 after you place your trade order. You will not get filled on this trade and your limit order will remain open. If the EUR/USD rate rises to 1.1300, then you will get filled on this trade but you will not get filled at a price of 1.1303.

The ability to place limit orders is recommended for those who are new to trading because it allows them to enter a market at the price they want. However, traders should be aware that the downside is that they may not get filled on their trade if the price does not go up or down enough for them to get filled at their desired entry point.

Also, remember that in some markets like forex and futures, there are requirements for placing limit orders and market orders. For example, many forex brokers require traders to place their orders in lots of 100 units or more while some futures brokers require traders to place their orders in increments of 10 or more contracts. Therefore, before placing a trade order with your broker, make sure you understand what is required of you when placing an order with them.

There are other types of trade orders that you can use to automate your trades but they are not available on all trading platforms. These include trailing stops and stop-limit orders.

3. Trailing Stops

A trailing stop is an order that is set to close your trade when the price moves a certain amount away from your entry price. This is different from a market order because a trailing stop will only be activated if the price of an asset moves in your favor.

A trailing stop can be placed on any open trade and it is usually used when you have open trades on assets that are trending in your favor. For example, if you have bought a stock and the stock has gone up significantly since then, you can place a trailing stop on your long position to lock in more profits.

When using trailing stops, there are two main types: Up-Ticks Trailing Stops and Down-Ticks Trailing Stops. The difference between these two types is the amount of movement that triggers the trailing stop to close out your trade. An Up-Ticks Trailing Stop closes out your position when the price moves up or down by one tick. A Down-Ticks Trailing Stop closes out your position when the price moves up or down by two ticks.

You should decide which type of trailing stop you want to use based on how much profit potential you have left with a particular trade and also how volatile the market is.

For example, if you have an Up-Ticks Trailing Stop set on your long position, the price of the asset has to move up by one tick for your order to be activated. If it moves down by one tick, your trailing stop will not be activated because the market has not moved in enough of a direction to trigger your trailing stop. However, if you have a Down-Ticks Trailing Stop set up on your long position, then the price of the asset will need to move down by two ticks for you to be activated. If the price of the asset moves up or stays at its current price, then your trailing stop will not be triggered and you will keep your trade open as usual.

When deciding on what type of trailing stop to use for an open trade, it is important that you have a good sense of how volatile that asset is and how close it is to reaching a potential support or resistance level. You also need to determine how much profit potential is left with your trade because there are times when choosing between either an Up-Ticks or Down-Ticks Trailing Stop can make all the difference in locking in maximum profits from a trade.

4. Stop-Limit Orders

A stop-limit order is used to automate your trades by placing a limit order that will be activated once the price reaches a certain price point or within a specified time. This type of trade order is useful for market conditions where prices have been moving so much that placing a limit order at the current market price may result in having your trade filled at a less than favorable price.

If you place an ordinary limit order, you can choose to set your desired price level for when your trade will be filled. You can also choose to set a time limit on your trade. However, with a stop-limit order, you do not need to select both of these options because this type of trade order automatically sets both conditions.

For example, if you place an ordinary limit order with the price of EUR/USD set at 1.1350 and with a time limit of 10 minutes, then this means that when the EUR/USD rate reaches 1.1350 within 10 minutes from now, then the system will place an automatic buy (or sell) at 1.1350 in an attempt to fill your open position and close out your position without you having to do anything else during these 10 minutes.

The advantage of using stop-limit orders is that you will not be forced to enter a market at an unfavorable price. The downside of using stop-limit orders is that you will not be able to see the price that your limit order is going to be filled at when placing the order.

This means that if the price moves up or down before your limit order is activated, then your trade may be filled at a price that you do not want and it may result in you losing out on potential profits.

Trading is all about making your money work harder for you. It is a way to generate a passive income by automating the trading process and letting the market go to work for you. In this section, we have discussed various types of trade orders and how you can use them to automate your trading.

Chapter 2: Stocks

In this chapter, you will learn all about stocks and investing in stocks. Stocks is perhaps the most well-known form of investing.

Stock market has been around for centuries and it has made a lot of people millionaires. Warren Buffet is perhaps the most notable stock investor in the world. He made his fortune by investing in stocks.

But that's not all, there are also countless other famous people who made their fortunes through investing in stocks.

It is no surprise then that investing in stocks is one of the most popular forms of investment around the world.

What is the stock market?

The stock market is a place where stocks are bought and sold.

There are many stock exchanges around the world. There is the New York Stock Exchange, London Stock Exchange, Hong Kong Stock Exchange, Shanghai Stock Exchange and others. The roles of these places are basically the same: to connect buyers and sellers of stocks.

The stock exchange that a particular stock is traded on decides how popular that stock is. For example, American stocks are usually traded on the New York Stock Exchange while Japanese stocks are generally traded in Tokyo.

But there are also many other exchanges such as the Nasdaq, Toronto Stock Exchange, Euronext etc. Each year, billions of dollars flow into these exchanges and out of these exchanges. There have been many studies conducted on the performance of stocks and it has been found that some countries perform better than others in terms of their stock market returns.

In addition, there are also clearing houses, which ensure that the stock market operates smoothly. They support the stock markets with their infrastructure and ensure that there are enough buyers and sellers of stocks.

There are also stock brokers who execute trades through the stock exchanges on behalf of their customers.

What is a stock?

A stock is a certificate that represents ownership of a company. This ownership is represented by stock shares.

When you purchase 1 share of Amazon, you own a small part of the company. It means that if Amazon does well in the future, you will get a part of the profit. That profit will be in the form of dividends paid to you as the owner.

You can also sell your share at any point in time if you wish to exit your holdings and earn some money as a result, or if you want to exit without making a loss, this is called short selling. Short selling is when you borrow shares from someone else and sell them on the market so that if they go down in price, you are able to buy them back at an even lower price and return them to their rightful owner.

You can think of this as betting against the stock market, but it's really just a way for people who do not want to buy stocks or hold onto them for long periods of time (for example people who want to make money quickly) can still make money on stocks without having to buy and hold onto stocks for long periods of time while they wait for their prices to rise again.

In fact, this is probably the most common way that stocks are bought and sold on the stock market.

Why do companies issue stock?

When a company wants to raise money, they issue stock to raise money.

A company can raise money by selling stocks. The company will issue some number of stocks and sell them to investors for cash.

The company will then use this cash to fund their operations or make investments and grow their business further.

This is also known as raising capital for the company. This is a very common way for companies to fund their expansion plans and grow even larger. This is why so many companies rely on investors who will purchase large numbers of stocks from the companies and give them cash for a period of time so that they can use that cash to fund their growth plans or other operations that require cash.

Of course, if you are one of these investors, you are hoping that the stock prices go up in value over time so that you can sell them at a profit later on. If they do, then you can make money off your investment since your initial investment will be worth more than when you bought it from the company initially. If not, then your investment goes down in value and you lose money as a result since your initial investment becomes worth less than what you invested in it initially — so if it goes down in value you lose money.

The different types of stocks

There are a few different types of stocks in the stock market. These types of stocks are as follows.

1. Common stocks

Common stocks are the most basic type of stock that you can purchase. They represent ownership in a company, and as such, they can be sold at any time for their market price (which is also called the fair market price of the stock).

If you own 1,000 shares of Amazon, then you own 1% of the company and will receive one dollar for every 10 dollars that Amazon earns. This is called a dividend.

2. Preferred stocks

Preferred stocks are stocks that have some special rights over common stocks. For example, preferred stock owners have their dividends paid first before common stockholders, or are guaranteed to get a certain amount of money each year that they do not have to pay back to the company if the value of their shares fall below a certain price.

3. Warrants

Warrants are a similar type of stock to preferred stocks, however they do not confer ownership. They are simply contracts that give the right to buy common stock at a certain price in the future.

Warrants are often issued by companies to reward employees or investors when they purchase common stock. This is how many big companies reward their employees for doing good work (by giving them warrants). It is also how some big investors make money on stocks. If someone invests in a company, and then that company goes public and issues more shares, the investor can use his warrants to buy new shares at a low price when the company goes public and make a lot of money when the value of those shares eventually increases over time.

What are Dividends?

Dividends are a form of profit that is paid out to the stockholders. It is basically what you will earn if you own a share of stock. The company will pay you in the form of dividends, depending on how much profit they make in a given year.

This is most common for stocks of companies that are established.

For example, if you own 1 share of Amazon, the company will divide its profit among all the shareholders. If you have 1 share of Amazon, you will get 1/1000th of Amazon's net income (profit). If the company earns $1 billion in profit that year and has 100 million shares outstanding, each shareholder will earn $10 per share as a dividend.

This is a pretty small amount right now, but if you owned 100 shares of Amazon, you would earn $1,000 in dividends.

To be clear, it's not a guarantee that you will earn dividends each year. If Amazon makes less profits in a given year, you won't earn any dividends for that year. You can only earn dividends if the company earns profits and if there is no priority for the company to pay out extra money to shareholders than it will pay out as a dividend.

Dividends are usually paid out at the end of a year, although they are not always paid out like this. You should always check with the company's website to see if they have declared dividends for that year and if so, how much they have been paid out. In many cases, companies will declare large dividends and then pay them out in installments over time.

What are stock splits?

A stock split is when a company increases the number of shares outstanding. In this way, each share will be worth less but there will be more shares of the company in circulation.

For example, if Amazon had 1000 shares outstanding and then did a 2 for 1 stock split, it would have 2000 shares outstanding but each share would be worth half of what they were before the stock split. This means that if Amazon earns $1 billion this year, then you would earn $5 per share instead of $10 per share.

There are several reasons why companies do this:

It becomes cheaper to purchase additional shares for people who want to invest in the company. This could potentially increase the price of a company's stocks over time as more and more people buy into it. There are also fewer total shares outstanding which makes it easier for investors to calculate how much profit each person will get per share as a dividend. It can also make a company's stocks seem more appealing to investors who want to calculate their valuation and how much money they should make in dividends over time by buying into their stocks. For example, if you owned 20% of the company before the stock split and now after the stock split you own 20% of the company, you will make 20% more money in dividends.

Usually, when the company has made the announcement, the price action on the stock will also increase. For example, if the price per share of Amazon was $500 before the stock split and then after the stock split, the price per share is $250, investors can easily see that they have doubled their money by purchasing more shares at a lower price.

How to categorize companies in the stock market

We can categorize companies based on their size, their business and other factors.

For our purpose, we will look at companies based on their size because it is the most important factor. Let's take a look at the different categories.

1. Blue Chips

Blue Chip companies are the largest and most profitable companies in the world. These companies are often household names and have been around for decades. Blue chips are known to be very stable and have a long history of providing good returns to investors.

The biggest blue chip companies include companies such as Apple, Amazon, Google, Facebook, Microsoft and more. These companies have the characteristics of having stable and predictable business, strong financials and are generally managed by very renowned leaders.

Blue chips are the best companies to invest in and if you are a beginner, I would recommend you to start with blue chip companies.

However, if you are looking for some volatility and growth potential, you should look at the next category.

2. Mid Caps

Mid cap companies are smaller companies that aren't as large as blue chips but they are bigger than micro caps. Mid caps are also generally more volatile than blue chips and micro caps. You can find mid cap companies whose stock prices have gone up by several thousand percent in a few short years.

Mid caps have the potential to give you huge returns but they could also fall by 90% in a few months or years. These companies are not as stable and predictable as blue chips but sometimes, you get more bang for your buck with mid cap companies compared to blue chips.

A good example of this is Microsoft which was once a mid cap company that has scaled to a blue chip over the years. Microsoft's stock price went from being around $5 per share in 1999 to around $100 per share today, representing a 5000% rise! Now, it trades at around $90 per share after scaling back in price over the last few years due to recent events. Today, Microsoft is now considered a blue chip company.

3. Small Caps

Small cap companies are the smallest companies in the stock market. They are generally very volatile and risky but can give you the biggest returns if you pick them right.

Small cap companies can multiply their stock price by 3,000% in a few years. However, they could also go bankrupt within a few years after going public. It is very risky to invest in small cap companies but if you are looking for growth potential and high returns, this is the category for you.

4. Micro Caps

Micro cap companies are the smallest companies in the stock market. These companies are very volatile and risky with small capitalization. These companies are also called penny stocks and they are very risky. They are risky as they are susceptible to fraud and mismanagement.

These types of companies have been known to go bankrupt within months of going public. However, if you pick one of these companies correctly, they can make you a lot of money as well. In addition, their small market capitalization would also mean that the price action would be very volatile given that a relatively smaller volume of trade orders can cause the price to move significantly.

As a beginner retail trader, I would not recommend you to invest in micro cap companies unless you have a lot of money to risk.

How are stock prices determined?

When people invest in stocks, they are actually buying shares of a company. For example if you buy 100 shares of Apple, you own 1% of Apple.

The price is determined by the earnings of the company and its future prospects. A company that has an awesome future will be valued more highly than a company that doesn't have a good future.

If you invest in stocks, your goal is to buy low and sell high. You want to buy stocks when they are cheap and sell them when they are expensive. That way you can make money even if the value doesn't increase much over time.

That's why buying stocks when they are cheap is very important. To do that you need to know how to read stock charts and other technical analysis tools. These tools will help you to find cheap stocks that have great potential for growth in price over time.

The price of the stocks can be influenced by several factors. The most important factor is the earnings of the company.

If the earnings are good then the stock price will go up and vice versa.

There are many other factors that influence stock prices. For example, if there is a war going on in a nation that produces a certain product, then the demand for that product will decrease and the stock price of the company will go down.

The valuation of a stock

The price of a stock can be calculated several ways. The most common way is to divide the company earnings by the number of shares.

For example, if a company has an earnings of 100$ and there are 100 shares outstanding, then you will know that the stock price is $1 per share.

Generally, stocks are valued on a per share basis. But they can also be valued on a market capitalization basis. Market capitalization is the total value of all outstanding shares in a company divided by the total number of outstanding shares in a company. That's why it is also called market cap.

For example, let's say that there are 10 million shares outstanding and the stock price is $10 per share then you know that the market capitalization is $100 million dollars for this company.

If there are just 500 shares outstanding then you will know that the market capitalization is $100 million because you divide 500 by 500 to get 1 and then you multiply it by 10 to get $10 million as market capitalization for this company.

You can calculate market capitalization as follows: (Number of Outstanding Shares x Stock Price) / Total number of Outstanding Shares in the Company.

The Risk/Reward of a stock

The risk/reward of a stock is the ratio between the amount you can make and the amount you can lose. This goes hand-in-hand with setting up stop losses.

If the reward is high then the risk should be low. If the reward is low then the risk should be high. The reward and risk are two sides of the same coin. Remember that stop losses are important to set up when you invest in stocks.

Stop losses are used by retail traders as well as professional traders. Professional traders use stop losses to minimize their market risk. Retail traders use stop losses to prevent themselves from losing money in a bad trade. It helps them to automatically cut their losses by triggering trade orders when certain conditions are met, such as when the stock price falls below a certain level. Most online trading platforms have an inbuilt feature where you can set up stop losses.

Most inexperienced retail traders let their emotions affect their trading decisions. They get greedy and they don't use stop losses. As a result, they lose money.

If you want to be successful in stocks, you must learn to control your emotions when you invest in stocks. When you buy a stock, don't wait for it to go up before selling it. Don't wait for the price to come back up before buying the next stock.

Always set up clear strategies and know what you are going to do when a trade goes against you. If it is a bad trade then cut your losses quickly and move on. Use stop losses to cut your losses automatically if things go against you. If it is a good trade then take profits early and then move onto the next trade if there are more good trades available at that time of day or week or month.

How do traders buy and sell stocks?

Retail investors like yourself can buy and sell stocks via a broker. They will charge you a fee for each transaction you make.

You can also sometimes buy and sell stocks directly without using a broker. This is called "direct trading" or "OTC trading". These are usually done by institutions such as banks, hedge funds, mutual funds etc. But retail investors can also do it occasionally if they wish to do so.

You can also buy and sell stocks through a custodian. However, you will not directly own the stocks. Instead, the custodian will hold the stocks for you under their name.

Specialized investment funds such as a hedge fund or a mutual fund can also invest in stocks. The advantage is that they don't have to buy and sell stocks individually. They can just do it as a group.

But they also face the same risk as individual investors. That's because they are just individual investors who pool their money together to invest in various companies. These investment decisions are not controlled by the individual investors of the fund, but by an appointed fund manager, who is in charge of the operations of the fund.

Chapter 3: Futures

I'm sure that you have heard "Futures" or "Futures Trading" a lot in the financial news media. You may have also seen "Futures Contracts" priced on a company's stock price. However, most of us have no idea what they are or how they work. In fact, most people ask themselves, "What are futures?" and "What are futures contracts?"

In this chapter, we are going to help you to understand what futures are and how they work.

What is the futures market?

The futures market is the market that provides a venue for traders to trade futures contracts, either cash-settled or physical-delivery.

A futures market can be organized or unorganized. An organized futures market has a central clearing house that acts as the counterparty to all contracts and guarantees all contracts. An unorganized futures market does not have a central clearing house and there are no guarantees behind any of its contracts.

The futures market is known to be very liquid. This means that it has large volume traded per day and can be easily accessed through different markets.

The futures market is also known to provide a more transparent market for information. This is because all futures contracts are standardized. Therefore, a trader can use complete information to make their trades without having to worry about hiding information from each other like in the stock market.

Many Hedge Funds use futures as a hedging tool. This means that they use futures contracts to reduce risk associated with price fluctuations in an underlying asset of their portfolio.

What is a futures contract?

Futures are an agreement to buy or sell an asset at a specified price at a specified future date. Futures are used by farmers, manufacturers and others to reduce the risk of price fluctuations in their cost of production. Futures also allow investors to speculate on the price movement in their chosen asset. This asset class is for traders with a higher level of risk appetite.

The futures market is used to hedge risk and prevent the possibility of a change in the price of the underlying asset having an adverse effect on the company. The futures market is also used for speculation to make a profit when the price goes up or down.

The futures market allows investors to take positions on assets which may not be available as shares or stocks. For example, if you wanted to trade corn, but this commodity is not traded on the stock exchange, you could use the corn futures market instead.

Futures are traded on exchanges, which operate similarly to stock exchanges. There are futures exchanges which specialize in particular assets, such as agricultural commodities or financial assets.

There are two types of futures contracts - calls and puts. A call is a long position, where you buy the right to buy an asset at a specified price in the future. A put is a short position, where you buy the right to sell an asset at a specified price in the future.

The futures market works in a similar way to the cash market, but instead of dealing with actual physical goods, investors trade financial derivatives called futures contracts. The futures market is used by those who want to take a long or short position on whether an asset will go up or down in price.

Traders buy and sell futures contracts with the hope of making a profit when the prices of futures contracts move in their favor. If you buy a futures contract, you are hoping the price will go up. If you sell a futures contract, you are hoping it will go down.

What are the different types of futures contracts?

There are 2 types of futures contracts:

1. Cash-settled futures contracts

These are futures contracts that have a settlement price. In this type of contract, the seller commits to selling the underlying commodity at a predetermined price. When the contract expires, the buyer is obligated to buy it at a predetermined price.

For example, if you buy a "March wheat" futures contract on the Chicago Mercantile Exchange (CME) you are committing yourself to purchase 5,000 bushels of wheat at $6.95 per bushel, by March. When the contract expires, the seller is obligated to sell you 5,000 bushels of wheat at $6.95 per bushel. The seller will just pay you the difference between the price that he is selling the wheat for and the price that you paid for it.

2. Physical-delivery futures contracts

These are futures contracts that have a physical settlement price. In these contracts, the buyer actually takes delivery of the commodity when the contract expires.

For example, if you buy a "June wheat" futures contract on the CME, you are committing yourself to purchase 5,000 bushels of wheat at $5.75 per bushel by June. When the contract expires, you take delivery of 5,000 bushels of wheat at $5.75 per bushel. The seller will be required to ensure that they have actual stock of the commodity.

As a retail trader, you will only need to worry about cash-settled contracts.

How do traders buy and sell futures contracts?

When traders buy or sell futures contracts, they expect to benefit from the difference between the current price of the underlying commodity and the price that they agree with the seller or buyer to pay.

Since the futures market is very large, it is not possible for each trader to buy and sell physical commodities. So, after traders make their cash-settled transaction, the CME arranges for a counterparty that will pay them when they are due to be paid and collect from them when they are due to make a payment.

Most retail traders will have to go through a broker to trade futures. The broker will arrange for a counterparty or hedge fund to do the same.

How are future prices determined?

That is an easy question to answer. The price of a futures contract is determined by supply and demand. However, this does not mean that the price of a futures contract is as high as the current price of the commodity or as low as the current price of the commodity.

Let's say, for example, that you want to buy a June wheat futures contract at $5.75 per bushel on the CME. In order for you to buy 5,000 bushels at $5.75 per bushel, somebody else must be willing to sell 5,000 bushels at that price. But if you are committed to buying 5,000 bushels at $5.75 per bushel by June and somebody else is also committed to selling 5,000 bushels at $5.75 per bushel by June, then there will be no trade!

How can we solve this problem? We can either increase or decrease the demand for wheat futures contracts until it matches with supply of wheat contracts in June 2017 (when the contract expires). If we need more wheat contracts in order for you to buy 5,000 contracts, then we will need to increase the demand for wheat contracts; if we need less wheat contracts, then we will need to decrease the demand for wheat futures contracts.

The only way that we can increase or decrease the supply and demand for a futures contract is by increasing or decreasing the price of the commodity. In other words, if we want to increase demand for wheat futures contracts, then we need to increase the price of wheat. If we want to decrease demand for wheat futures contracts, then we need to decrease the price of wheat. The same applies if we want to increase or decrease supply for a futures contract.

In a nutshell, increased demand for a futures contract leads to increased price and decreased demand for a futures contract leads to decreased price. Increased supply leads to decreased price and decreased supply leads to increased prices.

The valuation of a future contract

In order to value a future contract, you have to look at the underlying asset. For the most part, futures are valued based on the price of the actual commodity that is being traded. However, there are some contracts that are priced differently.

For example, in some cases, the price of gold and oil futures can be affected by factors other than the price of gold or oil itself. One such factor is supply and demand. For instance, if a political crisis in an oil-producing country leads to concern that supplies might be disrupted in the future, that could affect the price for oil futures. Similarly, if there is concern that demand for oil might increase over time due to economic growth or a change in consumer habits (like if people start buying more cars), that could also cause an increase in prices.

The futures market also has something called basis contracts. A futures basis contract allows someone to hedge their risk when investing in commodities like grains or metals. In order to understand how a basis contract works, it's important to know what basis means first. The term is often used as a benchmark for determining when there is more of one type of commodity available than another type. For example: If you want to buy wheat and there's already a ton of it in storage, it might be a bad time to invest because the price of wheat could go down. However, if you are trying to sell wheat and there is less of it on the market, that might be a good time to sell. In order to figure out how much wheat is available on the market, you can look at the basis.

When it comes to futures markets, basis refers to how much difference there is between the price of a commodity (like gold or oil) and its futures contract. Because those two prices are usually very close to each other, the basis isn't typically a big factor in determining whether or not an investor should buy or sell a futures contract. However, if there is enough of a gap between those prices (like when supply or demand for that commodity changes), then that could affect your decision about whether or not you want to buy or sell futures contracts for that commodity.

The Risk/Reward of a future contract

Understanding the Risk/Reward of a future contract is important because it will help you determine whether or not you are getting a good deal for your money. The risk/reward ratio is a way to measure how much money you can potentially lose versus how much money you can potentially make from your investment.

For example: let's say there is a futures contract for soybeans that costs $8,000 and will expire in 5 months. Let's also say that if the price of soybeans goes up by 1 cent then the futures trader would make about $400 USD. However, if the price goes down by 1 cent then the trader could lose about $400 USD. In this case, the Risk/Reward ratio would be 1:4 (1 to 4). That means that a trader has one chance in four of losing $400 each time they invest in a soybean futures contract. They have four chances in four of making $400 each time they invest in this contract (so their potential reward is 4x as much as their potential risk).

In addition, you have to remember that the futures trader will have to pay fees to buy the contract and they could also end up losing money due to price fluctuations. So even if they make $400 on a certain trade, they might not see that money because of the cost of buying the contract, or losses on their other trades.

So the Risk/Reward ratio can be really helpful in determining whether or not a futures trader is getting a good deal. If you think about it, it's kind of like gambling (which is why there are so many comparisons between trading and gambling). If you go into a casino and there are only 1:4 odds of winning, then pretty much everyone has an incentive to quit playing (unless you are stupid or just really enjoy being punished by Lady Luck). However, if you are playing at a casino where there are really good odds say 10:1 odds of winning then some people might be willing to stay at the table longer.

The Risk/Reward ratio can also help determine what types of strategies are best for traders. For instance: If someone knows that they have three chances in four of making $400 each time they invest in soybean futures contracts, but one chance out of four that they could lose $400, then they should only trade when they see a good opportunity. They might not want to invest in soybean futures if the market is already moving down and they don't have a good chance of making any money.

Also, one of the things that makes trading futures contracts a bit more complicated than some other types of trading is that there are many other factors involved.

For example: the price of the underlying commodity is just one factor that affects futures contracts. There are so many others as well: such as supply and demand, supply chain risk, political risks, hedging against currency fluctuations, and even how much it's going to cost you to buy or sell a certain contract. In order to make an educated decision about whether or not you want to buy or sell a futures contract, you need to consider all these factors and weigh them against each other. In order for your decision process as a trader to be successful, it's important that you take into account all of these factors.

Chapter 4: Forex

Forex, or Foreign Exchange, is a trade in which one country's currency is exchanged for another. It is the largest financial market in the world. In fact, it is estimated that 1.5 trillion USD worth of currency trades take place each and every day! Most of the trading is done electronically, with currency being traded on the New York Stock Exchange, the London Stock Exchange, and the Tokyo Stock Exchange. Most trades are executed by computer programs that are designed to spot patterns in the market and buy and sell currency automatically based on what they read.

The Forex market is extremely liquid, meaning that it is easy to execute a trade and the market is very active. In fact, it is estimated that there are over 500 million active traders in the Forex market! The market also offers an opportunity to realize high returns on investment, which is why there are so many investors worldwide.

While the Forex market has been around for a long time, it has only recently been introduced to the internet. In fact, the internet has made it easier than ever to trade, and more people are now investing in Forex than ever before.

While there are lots of advantages to trading in the Forex market, it is important for investors to understand what they're getting themselves into. This is why we're here: to tell you everything you need to know about trading in the Forex market!

What is a currency pair?

A currency pair is the two currencies that are being traded. For example, if you buy EUR/USD, then you are buying Euros and selling US Dollars.

The first currency of the pair is called the base currency, and the second is called the quote currency. In this case, EUR/USD means that Euros are being exchanged for US Dollars.

It is important to note that in order to buy or sell a pair, you must first buy or sell one of the currencies in it. So if you want to make a trade in USD/CAD, then you must first sell CAD to get USD. Once you have USD, you can then buy CAD with it!

Here are the major currency pairs in the world:

- EUR/USD (Euros vs. US Dollars)
- JPY/USD (Japanese Yen vs. US Dollars)
- GBP/USD (British Pounds vs. US Dollars)
- AUD/USD (Australian Dollars vs. US Dollar)
- CHF/USD (Swiss Francs vs. US Dollar)
- NZD/USD (New Zealand Dollar vs. US Dollar)

These currency pairs are referred to as majors, and they are the most widely traded currency pairs in the Forex market.

Here are some of the minor currency pairs:

- GBP/CHF (British Pound vs. Swiss Franc)
- AUD/NZD (Australian Dollars vs. New Zealand Dollar)
- JPY/CNH (Japanese Yen vs. Chinese Yuan)
- CAD/CHF (Canadian Dollar vs. Swiss Franc)

These pairs are not as widely traded, but they are still used in the Forex market.

The currency pairs above are all considered to be "major" currency pairs because they have a lot of volume and liquidity in the market. This means that there are a large number of buyers and sellers, which makes it easy to get into and out of trades quickly. On the other hand, some pairs may not have as much volume or liquidity, meaning that they may take longer to get into or out of trades!

However, trading in them can also be profitable! The choice is up to you!

How are currencies traded on the forex market?

On the Forex market, currency is traded in pairs. This means that one unit of currency is traded against another unit of a different type of currency. For example, a trade may involve exchanging the US dollar for the British Pound. This is a pair trade and it involves exchanging 2 different currencies. The first currency in the pair will be called the base currency and the second will be called the quote currency. The base currency will always be worth more than the quote currency! This is because it is relatively easy to buy and sell base currencies, while it can be harder to buy and sell currencies that are not so popular.

Forex is by far the most liquid market in the world as there is always a bid and ask price on each currency pair. This means that there is always someone willing to buy or sell at any price! This is what makes trading in the Forex market so attractive – it is very liquid and easy to get started!

As long as the world is trading between its different currencies, then the Forex market will be around for a very long time!

Who controls the forex markets?

The Forex market is controlled by many different entities. Central banks are the most obvious leaders, and they set the exchange rates for their respective currencies. For example, the US Federal Reserve is the central bank of the United States. They are responsible for setting the value of American currency and determining what it's worth against other currencies.

In order to manage their currencies, central banks have their own trading desks that are responsible for buying and selling on behalf of their governments. These trading desks have very large amounts in assets, which means that they can buy and sell lots of currency at any given time. In order to manage these assets, central banks will hire traders who will execute trades on behalf of their governments.

There are also large corporations that trade on a daily basis. These companies often buy and sell based on supply and demand in the market, which means that they might buy a ton of currency when there is a shortage or sell them when there is an excess! This can cause fluctuations in the price of a single unit, but it isn't all bad news! The more people who trade currencies, then more people will be interested in trading currency pairs!

There are also retail traders who trade on a daily basis. These traders are often the largest traders in the world because they can buy and sell currency in very large quantities. In fact, many retail traders can even trade on margin, which means that they can borrow money from the bank to fund their trades. This means that lots of retail traders have access to large amounts of capital and they often trade with it!

Just like the big corporations, retail traders are looking to profit from fluctuations in currency exchange rates, which means that they will buy when there is a shortage and sell when there is an excess! This is a great way for a trader to make money over time, but it also makes it difficult to predict what will happen next!

What are the main technical indicators used for trading on the forex market?

In order to understand what technical indicators are, one must first understand what a chart is. A chart is a graphical representation of the price of an asset plotted over time. Charts are used for analyzing a market or forecasting its future path.

Technical indicators are used for measuring the current state of the market and finding trends that will allow you to predict where prices might go in the future.

There are several categories of indicators, which can be broken down into three main types: trend-following, mean-reversion, and oscillators.

Trend-following indicators attempt to predict future price movement by identifying if an asset is trending up or down over time in order to determine a possible entry point. Some popular trend-following indicators include Moving Average Convergence Divergence (MACD) and Average True Range (ATR)

Mean-reversion indicators attempt to identify trends before they begin so that you can determine when to get in on them before they start moving in the opposite direction. Some popular mean-reversion indicators include Bollinger Bands and Parabolic SAR.

Oscillators represent both prices and time in relation to one another. Oscillators can be plotted on the same chart as price but are usually used together with other indicators to help determine future price movement. Some popular oscillators include Relative Strength Index (RSI), Chaiken Oscillator, and Stochastic Oscillator (STO).

The risk/return of trading currencies using technical analysis

When investing in Forex, there are a couple of things to consider. The first is that the Forex market is extremely liquid. This means that it is easy to execute a trade, and that the market is very active. In fact, it is estimated that there are over 500 million active traders in the Forex market! What this also means is that the market is extremely volatile. In fact, it has been known to fluctuate by over hundreds of points in a single day.

Since the Forex market is very liquid and very volatile, investors get to see large returns on their investment. While this is great for investors, it also means that they are taking on more risk than they may realize. This is because currencies can trade down as well as up!

The Forex market can be a very exciting place to invest, but it's important to remember that there are risks involved. For those who want to take on more risk in order to make larger gains, the Forex market is an excellent choice. However, those who want a more stable investment should probably consider trading elsewhere!

Most retail traders will be introduced to margin trading for forex by their online trading platforms. Increasing leverage is available on all retail forex broker platforms. Leverage allows traders to trade more currency with the same amount of cash. This is because a deposit that is used to open a position does not have to be held in reserve by the broker or platform. It can be used as collateral instead.

While retail forex brokers usually allow you to trade with 100% leverage or more, they do limit your total exposure, and this is where the margin requirement comes into play.

Many retail forex brokers have a minimum margin requirement for opening a trade. This will be the same amount of money that you must deposit into your account when you open a position. This will ensure that if the price of the currency moves against you, you will have enough capital to cover your losses.

You may also have to have more than a minimum margin requirement in order to maintain the trade. Your broker may require that you maintain a certain amount of equity in your account. This is because, as we mentioned earlier, it is possible for the price of the currency to move against you while you are holding it. If this happens, the broker can close out your positions for little or no loss to themselves. The difference between the buy and sell price can be used as collateral to keep your account from going into negative equity.

With some forex brokers, there are no limits on how much leverage you can use while trading currencies in real time markets or in intra-day markets (markets where trades take place within one day). However, leverage is limited on many retail forex platforms when it comes to trading currencies in longer-term contracts (forex calendar spreads).

The Risk/Reward of Forex Trading

As with most types of investment, the higher the risk, the larger the potential for return. The same is true of Forex trading. Currency values fluctuate constantly and can change rapidly in both positive and negative directions. When you buy a currency, you are speculating that its value will increase (or holding a position that has already done so).

When you sell a currency, you are speculating that its value will decrease (or closing out a position that has already done so). Because currencies can increase or decrease in value very quickly, your trades can have large gains or losses. These gains or losses are also referred to as profits or losses. This is because they are your profit or loss from trading your currency positions!

The risks involved in Forex trading are different than those in other types of investments such as stocks and bonds. In most types of investing, it is thought that past performance does not guarantee future results. This is because these investments tend to be more stable across time periods than currencies.

The key to making money when trading Forex is understanding which currencies are likely to change rapidly in value and which are not. It is also important to understand what drives the value of a currency up or down. This is because the factors that cause changes in the value of currencies will often be different than those that cause changes in other types of investments.

Forex trading can be very exciting and profitable, but it does have a high risk factor associated with it. However, understanding how to manage your risk and how to make money while trading Forex can help you get started making real money while trading in this exciting market!

How do traders make money trading currencies on the forex market?

In order for a trader to profit, they simply need to be able to buy and sell currencies at a rate that is higher than what they paid for them. If you buy one currency at $1 USD and sell it at $1.05 USD, then you have made $0.05 USD on your transaction. If you multiply this by the amount of transactions that you make per day, week or month, then you can see how profits can add up quickly!

There are several ways that retail traders can make money trading Forex:

They may be able to spot price trends in the market and profit from these trends by buying and selling currencies accordingly. This strategy is called "technical analysis" because it involves projecting future prices based on past patterns in the market. Traders may also be able to spot mispricings in the market and exploit these situations by buying a currency where it isn't as cheap as it should be (or selling a currency where it isn't as expensive as it should be).

Binary Options are another way that retail traders can make money trading Forex. Binary options are a type of financial "bet" that can be placed on any number of different Forex-related events. For example, you may be able to bet on the price of the EURO at a certain time in the future, or you may be able to bet on the price of gold over a certain period of time. The difference between binary options and conventional options is that binary options have one outcome: either you win or you lose the full amount of your bet. For example, if you were to place a $100 bet on gold rising in value during the next year, but gold actually decreased in value by $100 over that period of time, then you would have lost all of your money. Unlike conventional options where you could still make some money back.

What are the different types of orders?

As with any type of trading, it is important to understand the different types of orders that you can execute when trading in the Forex market. If you are not familiar with the different types of orders, it is recommended that you read over this section before continuing.

1. Market Order

A market order is an order to buy or sell currency at the best available rate. If you want to buy or sell a currency immediately, you can execute a market order. However, since the market never stops moving, it is possible that the price of your currency will be different when your trade is executed. This creates the risk of slippage, which means that you may not get the price you expected.

To avoid slippage, it is recommended that you use limit orders instead of market orders whenever possible. A limit order allows you to set a price for when your trade is executed.

2. Limit Order

A limit order allows you to set a specific price for when your trade will be executed. If the market moves beyond your set price, then your trade will not be executed! However, if the market moves in your favor and hits or surpasses your set range, then your trade will be executed right away! Limit orders are extremely useful for investors who want to execute trades without worrying about slippage or other factors that might affect their trades. The only problem with limit orders is that they take longer than market orders to execute and they have higher fees attached to them as well.

What is a pip?

When trading in the Forex market, it is important to know how much each currency trade will cost. The price of each trade is known as a pip. A pip is the smallest amount by which a currency pair can change. For example, if the exchange rate between EUR/USD is 1.2118/1.2116, then 10 pips have changed in favor of the Euro.

Different currency pairs have different pip values. For example, if USD/CAD changes from 1.3171 to 1.3172, then only one pip has changed in the value of the USD vs the CAD. Most analysis of forex price movements will be quoted in pips, so it is important that you understand what a pip is.

Why is the forex market so volatile?

Volatility means that a currency will rise and fall quickly or wildly. So we can say a currency is volatile when its value changes dramatically over short periods of time. The currency exchange rate for this reason will be more likely to experience rapid increases or decreases in price than other currencies that do not fluctuate as much as this one does. This means that there can be great opportunities for making money from trading if you know what you are doing! But you need to keep good records as well!

The forex market is so volatile because it is the largest financial market in the world. The US dollar is the world's most important currency, and around 40% of all foreign exchange transactions are made in US dollars.

All of these currency trades are made by banks and hedge funds, which use complex computer algorithms to place their orders. These algorithms are designed to make a profit every time there is a movement in the forex market price.

This constant placing of orders creates a huge amount of activity in the forex market, which drives prices up or down very quickly. This can cause dramatic changes in price, which makes the forex market very volatile.

What is High-Frequency Trading?

High-frequency trading is a type of trading that uses extremely fast and advanced computer trading systems to automatically generate trade signals. This system can be used for either buying or selling.

HFT uses very advanced algorithms to predict the movements of prices in the forex market. These algorithms are based on historical price data, and they can also be used for other types of cross-market analysis, such as real estate, commodities and more. HFT can make a profit from any movement in the price of a currency.

There are two types of high-frequency traders: one is called buy-side HFT, which normally makes its trades using its own capital; and the other is called sell-side HFT, which normally acts on behalf of investors rather than its own account. Both of these groups are making money every time there is a movement in a currency's price due to their knowledge about how the markets will react. When you find that you are making consistent profits from trading in these volatile markets, then you know it's time to expand your investment strategies to include other types of investments!

Currently, the majority of trading that takes place in the forex market is done with the use of high-frequency trading systems and other types of trading robots that use advanced computer algorithms to execute trades.

Retail traders like yourself can also make use of such trading robots, which are available in the form of trading software and online trading platforms, to trade in a more profitable way.

The forex market is one of the most difficult to trade, because it has such fast-paced movements. But if you can master the art of making money from this market, then there is no better place for you to invest your money! You can begin by learning how to use a forex trading robot!

Chapter 5: Bonds

When you ask most retail traders and investors what they think the safest investment is, the majority of them would say that bonds are the safest. Bonds have been the staple of investment portfolios for decades.

Most conservative investors would recommend that the majority of your investment portfolio be made up of bonds. They will even go as far to recommend that you have enough money saved up to where you can invest in bonds for at least ten years, if not more.

The reason many investors recommend having a long-term bond portfolio is because they are stable and they are typically considered safer than stocks.

In fact, when the stock market is down, investors often move their money into bonds for the short-term as a form of protection. The logic behind this is that when the stock market is down, the value of bonds tends to go up.

There are a few reasons why bonds tend to go up when stocks go down. One reason is that bonds are considered a lower risk investment than stocks.

Another reason is that investors will often buy up bonds when they think the economy is going to be bad in order to protect their assets. This typically occurs during times of war, economic downturns, and even when there are rumors of an economic collapse.

Bond prices tend to increase in times like these because investors will demand a higher rate of return for taking on the risk. This will drive the price of bonds up.

So are bonds really a safe investment? Or are they just something that is touted as being safe? Let's find out!

What is a Bond?

A bond is a debt instrument that is used for borrowing money. Bonds are like loans that pay interest and eventually get paid back with interest.

Think of bonds as an "IOU" that can be traded. It's basically a loan that is issued by a government entity or corporation. The issuer will issue bonds to investors for a specific amount of money in order to raise capital.

The issuer will charge the investor interest for borrowing their money. In return, they will pay the investor back with interest over time until they pay back the full amount of the loan with interest.

For example, if you invest $1,000 into a company's bond, they would charge you an interest rate of 5%. This means that in one year, you would have $1,050 in your account. In two years, your account would be worth $1,100 because you would be charged interest again. You would then receive this money at the end of year three when the bond reaches maturity and is paid back to you.

Many people think of bonds as being safer than stocks because there is no risk involved when trading them. No matter what the stock market or economy does, a bond will ALWAYS pay you back your principal investment with interest.

That means that if you invest $1,000 into a bond and it pays you 5% interest per year, you will receive your $1,000 back with another $50 in interest when the bond reaches maturity. That's why most investors prefer to invest in bonds rather than stocks. There is no risk involved when investing in bonds.

When stocks are down, bonds tend to go up because investors will buy them up for protection from the market declining. In this situation, the price of bonds goes up because investors demand more return on their investment for taking on that additional risk. This is known as a "flight to safety" mentality where investors move their money into investments that are considered safer than stocks because of market uncertainty.

Since bonds are considered a fixed-income investment, it means that the price you pay for them is fixed. In other words, the price of a bond does not fluctuate based on anything other than what the issuing entity charges you to borrow their money.

In fact, the only time a bond price will change is when the issuing entity decides to change its interest rate. If the interest rate goes higher, then it will cost you more money to buy that bond because they are charging more for their loan. If the interest rate goes lower, then it will cost you less money to buy that bond because they are charging less for their loan.

How are bonds issued?

The loan is usually issued by a government entity or a corporation. The corporation or government entity will issue bonds to investors in order to raise money for their operations.

In the case of a corporation, they will issue bonds to raise money for expansion purposes, such as buying new equipment, expanding production, or even raising capital through stock offerings.

Bonds can be issued in the form of paper at first, but they are typically transferred electronically now. This means that most bonds these days are purchased and sold through electronic trading systems, such as on the stock market, which is what we will be looking at today. It also means that most bond trades take place on your trading platform from your broker. This makes them very similar to stocks in terms of investing and trading them.

Bonds can be issued for a variety of reasons and they can also be issued by many different types of entities such as corporations and government entities. The main thing about bonds is that they always pay you your original investment back with interest over time until they mature and are paid back entirely at maturity. That's why most investors prefer them over stocks. You don't have to worry about your investment. It's almost 100% guaranteed.

However, there are times when the issuer of the bond defaults or goes bankrupt. This means that they will not be able to pay you back at maturity date, even if you are due your principal and interest payments.

But the good news is that there are also many government entities that exist to insure your investment in bonds. This means that there is very little risk when it comes to investing in bonds unless the issuing entity goes bankrupt or defaults on their bond payments.

When this happens, it is up to the government entity to step in and pay investors back. This is why most people prefer to invest in bonds because they are considered safer than stocks. There's no risk involved for them as long as you don't buy bonds from a failing or bankrupt company/government entity because they can always be insured by a government entity without defaulting on their payments.

The different types of bonds

There are two main types of bonds: Government Bonds and Corporate Bonds. Each has different characteristics, pros, and cons, which we will discuss shortly. First, let's look at how each form of bond is issued so we can better understand how they work and why they are issued in the first place.

1. Government Bonds:

Government Bonds are issued by a country's government to raise money for public projects, such as building a bridge or providing social security. The government will issue bonds in exchange for an investor lending them money. When you buy a government bond, you are essentially loaning the government money. When the bond matures, or is paid back, the government will pay you back your initial investment plus interest.

Usually, government bonds are known to be very safe investments. This is because the government itself is backing the bond, and it's considered a loan to the government. So, the government knows they have to pay you back at some point. In fact, governments will even bail out investors holding bonds in case of default or bankruptcy.

2. Corporate Bonds:

Corporate Bonds are issued by companies (instead of governments) to raise money for business projects. A company will issue bonds in exchange for an investor loaning them money. When you buy a corporate bond, you are essentially loaning a company money. When the bond matures or is paid back, you will receive your initial investment plus interest from the company.

Just like when you buy a government bond, when investing in corporate bonds you can choose to get paid interest either on a regular basis or all at once when the bond matures/is paid back. While corporate bonds are usually considered less risky than government bonds because they are backed by a company rather than a government, they can still be risky if the company goes bankrupt or defaults on paying investors back! Some reasons why this may happen include if there's an unexpected collapse in revenues for example, or drop in price of their product or service.

The maturity date of bonds

Bonds have a maturity date, which is the date that the bond will be repaid. This usually occurs after a number of years of paying interest to the investor. The length of time that interest is paid will vary from one bond to another but all will have a maturity date, which is known as the bond's duration.

Bonds issued by governments or government agencies typically have a term of 30 years. For businesses, bonds are typically issued with terms between 5-7 years.

When government and business debt is in high demand, the price of bonds will increase. For example, if the government issues a large amount of bonds to finance a war, the price of these bonds will rise because there is more supply while demand remains constant. This is because investors are willing to pay more for bonds with higher interest rates when there are a greater number of bonds that can be purchased.

When interest rates begin to fall, the prices of existing bonds will also fall. This is because investors do not want to pay as much for a bond that has an interest rate lower than those offered by new bonds.

The sensitivity of bond prices to changes in interest rates is known as the duration. The duration will vary based on what type of bond is being purchased but typically, long-term bonds have greater duration than short-term or medium term bonds.

The rating of bonds

Bonds are rated according to their perceived risk. Bonds that are backed by the government or government agencies will typically have a higher rating than those issued by a company.

The most common ratings for bonds are AAA, AA, A and BBB. The least risky bonds have a rating of AAA while those with the highest risk will have a rating of BBB. Those with a BBB rating are considered to be below investment grade and have an increased likelihood of defaulting on their payments.

The ratings are provided by rating agencies such as Moody's and Standard and Poors. These ratings are a measure of the ability of a government or company to repay their debts. If they are unable to repay their debts, they will default on their payments or file for bankruptcy.

Bonds issued by governments are considered to be the safest due to the fact that they can raise taxes in order to repay their debts should they need to do so. Bonds issued by companies can also be considered safe if the company is able to generate enough income in order to pay its debts when they become due.

Corporations have a lower rating than governments because they have a higher risk of defaulting on their bonds payments if they are not able to generate enough income in order to pay what is owed. This is especially true when corporations begin experiencing financial difficulties that result in them being unable to pay what is owed on time or at all for that matter.

The yield of a bond

The yield of a bond is simply the total return you can expect to receive by investing in that particular bond.

Some people refer to it as the coupon rate because it is the amount paid to you for loaning your money. It's also referred to as the gross yield because there are other factors that should be considered while calculating your net yield (your total return, or gain).

The total return of a bond can be calculated in three different ways:

Actual or Nominal Yield: This simply takes the interest rate on a bond and multiplies it by the price of a bond. So if you have a $1,000 par value bond with a 3% coupon, your actual yield is $30.

Compounded Annual Yield: This takes your actual or nominal yield and adds the effect of compounding. Compounding means that you earn interest on both your initial investment and also on your interest earnings over time. So let's take our example above. If we had invested $1,000 into this particular bond, compounded annually our total gain would be $37 ($30 x 1.085). This means we've earned an additional 8.5% in one year from our initial investment which isn't too bad. But this brings us to our last term:

Effective Annual Yield: This is the true picture of your total return. It takes compounded annual yield and then subtracts the price you paid for the bond. So let's take the same example from above. If we had purchased that $1,000 bond for $900, our effective annual yield would be $30 x 1.085 - ($900 x 1.085) = $36.31 which means a 3% return on our initial investment of $900 (or an additional total of 36%). If we had purchased our bond for $1,000, our effective annual yield would be $37, which means a 3% gain on an initial investment of $1,000 (or a total additional gain of 37%).

What factors affect the price of a bond?

When it comes to bond investing, there are many factors that may affect the price of a bond. Some of these factors include:

1. Time To Maturity

The longer the time to maturity, the greater the risk. If you invest in a 30 year bond, there is a chance that the bond issuer may default before the maturity date. However, the longer the time to maturity, the greater will be the interest rate. You will need to monitor the market to make sure that the current interest rate is at a level that you are willing to accept the risk of investing in a longer term bond.

2. Credit Rating

The credit rating of the country is one of the most important factors that affect the price of a bond. If you invest in a country whose credit rating is not good, there is a chance that there will not be enough buyers for your bond and it may become difficult to resell it in future. Hence, it is important to check the credit rating before investing in any bonds. The higher the credit rating, the greater will be your chances of getting good returns by purchasing bonds from companies with good ratings.

3. Federal Funds Rate

The Federal Funds Rate is one of the key rates that affect both short term and long term bonds. The Federal Funds Rate is decided by the US Fed Reserve Bank and it essentially states how much banks can lend each other on an overnight basis without any collateral or security. This rate has an impact on how much banks can lend to individuals and companies for loans as well as how much they have to pay when taking out loans from other banks. When this rate increases, companies and individuals will have higher borrowing costs and hence it becomes more expensive for the companies to issue bonds.

4. Inflation

The inflation rate is another factor that affects the price of bonds. If there is a high level of inflation, companies and individuals will have to pay more interest on their loans which in turn will increase their borrowing costs and hence they will have higher expenses. This in turn means that investors will not be able to get good returns on the bonds they own. Hence, it is important to monitor the inflation rate before investing in bonds as it can affect your bond investment greatly.

5. Duration

Duration is another key factor when it comes to bond investing. The duration of a bond is determined by the bond issuer's credit rating, interest rate and redemption value (in case you want to sell the bond earlier). The longer the duration of a bond, the greater your chances of getting higher returns due to reinvesting interest earned from previous years into newer bonds with high yields. However, if you invest in long term bonds, there is a risk of losing money if you are unable to resell them in future because there may not be enough buyers for your long term bonds due to an adverse market scenario or if you are not able to find any buyers at all. Hence, it is important to do careful research before investing in long term bonds.

The above factors are some of the main factors that affect the price of a bond. It is important to monitor these factors before you invest in bonds as they can have an impact on your bond investment.

The Risk/Reward of a bond

The systematic risk of bonds:

The systematic risk associated with bonds is less significant than it is with stocks. This is because the systematic risk of bonds is less likely to affect the bond price in a significant manner.

The systematic risk associated with bonds has to do with the economic health of the issuer. If an issuer is experiencing financial difficulties, they may be unable to repay their debts as scheduled. Although this does not happen often, it does happen on rare occasions.

For example, Greece was once considered to be one of Europe's strongest economies but in recent years, it has fallen into a severe recession that has resulted in it being unable to pay what was owed on some of its bonds and defaulting on others. This is an example of systematic risk impacting a bond's value in a negative manner though this type of impact is relatively rare compared to what occurs with stocks.

The event risk associated with bonds:

Bonds are also impacted by event risk such as government policy that results in interest rates being lowered or raised or changes in laws and regulations that make it more difficult for issuers to manage their debt obligations. For example, if the government reduces or increases taxes, this can have a positive or negative impact on the ability of governments and businesses to pay back what they owe their investors even though these types of changes typically do not have a great impact on bond prices.

The price of bonds is also impacted by event risk such as changes in interest rates that occur when a major economic event occurs. For example, if the government raises or lowers interest rates in order to promote economic growth, this can have a positive or negative impact on the price of existing bonds. This is because investors are more likely to purchase bonds with lower interest rates than those that have higher interest rates.

Similarly, if a company experiences financial difficulties and issues new bonds to raise capital, these new bonds will likely be issued with lower interest rates than those issued during better economic times. This will result in existing bondholders seeing their investment decline as the yield on their existing bond declines with the new issuance of debt securities.

The credit risk associated with bonds:

Credit risk refers to the likelihood that an issuer will default on its payments when they become due. The two major credit ratings agencies are Standard & Poors and Moody's which both provide ratings for corporate and government debt securities. These ratings are based on the likelihood of default taking into account factors such as GDP growth, inflation, tax revenues and other indicators of economic strength or weakness that may affect whether an issuer is able to pay its debts.

Bonds can be rated from AAA to C or below which refers to the likelihood of default. Bonds that are rated AAA are considered to be very unlikely to default whereas those that are rated below C have a much higher likelihood of defaulting. The lower the rating, the greater the likelihood that an issuer may default on its debt obligations.

The bond market is huge and most investors who purchase bonds do not worry about whether an issuer will be able to pay their debts when they become due but instead focus on the return investors can get from these investments. The return on bonds depends on both the credit rating of the issuer as well as what interest rate is being paid by these companies and/or governments. This means that if an investor purchases a bond with a low credit rating, they may only see their investment return when interest rates rise which is known as a capital gain and also means these investors could lose money if interest rates fall as this will result in them only receiving less income than expected.

The liquidity of bonds:

Liquidity refers to how easy it is to sell a bond for cash at any given time without losing money by doing so. Liquidity is high when there is a significant number of buyers and sellers for a particular security that are willing to buy or sell at any given time.

Bonds can be extremely difficult to sell as they tend to have long maturities which means that investors are forced to hold these securities for a long period of time. An investor may want to sell their bond if their investment strategy has changed or they need cash in order to purchase other securities. However, the bond market is not very liquid as most bonds cannot be sold on a daily basis and the process of selling bonds is relatively difficult with most major investors having access only to a small fraction of the total bond market at any given time.

In order to sell a security, an investor is forced to get in touch with the brokerage company they hold their bond with which will likely require them having access to a broker that specializes in selling bonds held by retail investors. This process can be lengthy as it takes time for the broker to find another buyer for this security who may be willing to pay what is being demanded by the seller or even more if they want this transaction completed quickly. This means that it often takes at least two weeks for an investor who wants to sell a bond they have purchased before they are able to do so and this can result in them losing money as interest rates go up or down in the meantime.

The trading of bonds is also more complicated than the trading of stocks and requires a great deal more knowledge and understanding than investors who only purchase stocks are likely to have. This means that relatively few investors are able to sell their bonds when they want to and they may be forced to sell them at a loss or wait until these securities can be sold at a profit which can take months if not longer.

The risk of default associated with bonds:

The risk of default is determined by the credit rating of an issuer. The higher the credit rating, the lower the likelihood that an issuer will default on its debts when they become due. As noted above, this is based on factors such as GDP growth, inflation, tax revenues and other economic factors that indicate whether an issuer will be able to pay their debts when they become due. The credit ratings from Standard & Poors and Moody's are often used by investors who want to determine whether a bond is likely to perform well or not before purchasing it. These ratings are often included by companies issuing bonds as part of their offering documents which makes it easier for investors to compare similar types of bonds from multiple issuers.

When would a trader buy bonds?

Traders buy bonds when there is a high level of uncertainty in the market and they feel that they can make more money by buying bonds from countries with good credit ratings, rather than investing in stocks and commodities. If stocks have fallen significantly and a trader wants to make some money from these falls, he may choose to invest in bonds instead as it may give him higher returns.

This is because while stocks give you a share of the profits of a company, bonds pay you interest based on the credit rating of a country and hence they may give you higher returns than stocks if you choose to buy bonds from countries with good credit ratings.

When would a trader sell bonds?

Traders sell bonds when they feel that interest rates are going to be increased in the near future and hence it is better to sell the bonds they own and invest their money in other investments that give them a higher return. This is because bonds are considered to be safer investments as compared to stocks and commodities, so if there is a risk that interest rates may increase in future, it is better to sell your bonds and invest in other investments for which you can get a higher return.

The above was a brief introduction on the factors that affect the price of bonds. If you are planning to invest in bonds, it is important for you to do careful research before investing in them as it can help you make wiser decisions.

Chapter 6: Options

In this chapter, we will be covering options. If you are familiar with stocks and futures, then options will be pretty easy to understand. This financial asset is called an option as it gives the holder the option to buy or sell an underlying asset at a specific price.

Options have been used to reduce risk, and they have been used as a way to take advantage of market movements. Options can be categorized into two groups, Call options and Put options.

What is the options market?

The market for options is a derivative market. In simple terms, that means it was created to allow traders to trade the price of an underlying asset without actually owning it.

The options market is primarily used for two purposes: Hedging and speculation.

Hedging is essentially insurance against price movements by limiting your risk exposure. If you own a substantial amount of an asset, you can hedge part of your position by selling call options. If the price of the underlying asset moves up and against your position, you will lose money on the option. However, if the underlying asset price moves in line with your position, you will profit from the option. This is why options are also used to speculate.

Options are contracts that give you (the buyer) the right to buy or sell an underlying asset at a specific price (the strike price) on or before a specific date (the expiry date). The seller of an option is known as an option writer. In return, the writer receives a premium for taking on that risk.

For example, let's say you think the price of gold will go up. You can buy a call option on the SPDR Gold Shares ETF. This gives you the right to buy 100 shares for $120 per share. However, if gold goes to $130 per share, you could exercise your right and sell your shares at $120 and make a profit of $10 per share ($130-$120).

The most obvious way to make money from options is to buy them and hold onto them until they expire. If you predict the movement of an underlying asset correctly, you will make a profit. If you don't, then unfortunately your options will expire worthless and you lose all of your money.

There are two strategies that are designed around profiting from option contracts: The long straddle strategy and the short straddle strategy. They work in very different ways (the long straddle strategy involves buying both puts and calls while the short straddle strategy involves selling both puts and calls), but they both focus on allowing traders to profit from volatility in an underlying asset price while limiting their risk exposure.

What is an option?

Options are a derivative of the underlying asset that helps in making profit for the trader, it is not a simple 'buy or sell' transaction where you buy and then wait for the price to increase. It is more like you are entering an agreement with the seller to purchase a particular quantity of the underlying asset at a predetermined price on or before a specified date.

Option contracts are of two types:

1. Call option

A call option is an agreement between the seller and the buyer to buy a specific quantity of the underlying asset at a predetermined price on or before a specified date. It is called a call because the owner of the option has the right but not the obligation to purchase a particular quantity of the underlying asset.

a. Put option

A put option is an agreement between the seller and the buyer to sell a specific quantity of the underlying asset at a predetermined price on or before a specified date. It is called a put because the owner of this option has the right but not obligation to sell a particular quantity of underlying asset.

How do traders buy and sell options?

Options contracts are traded through option exchanges. The main exchanges are the CBOE, CME and the ISE. If you have a brokerage account with a futures broker, it will most likely have access to one of these exchanges. You can also trade options on some cryptocurrency exchanges, including Kraken and Poloniex.

To buy or sell an option contract, you need to create an options account with an online broker who has access to one of these exchanges. You then place a market order for a call or put option. This allows you to buy or sell the option immediately at the current price based on the last trade price. If you want to enter your order at a different price, you will need to do this via an OTC (Over-The-Counter) broker who trades directly with other investors looking for options contracts at their desired price (known as "specialists").

The mechanics of entering orders can be confusing for new traders because there are several ways to do so depending on whether you want to buy or sell.

It is possible that traders will end up closing out positions with both exchange and OTC brokers if they hold long positions until expiration day when they will close out their position based on the strike price and take their profits.

What does it cost to trade options?

This depends on which brokerage you choose. Some brokers will charge a flat rate of $0.10 per contract while others will charge a percentage of the total contract value (known as "tape"). You should also be aware that the cost of selling an option is higher than buying an option. For example, if you buy an option for $1, you may only be able to sell it for $0.90 depending on market conditions, expiration date and whether the strike price is in-the-money or not. When you sell an option, you will need to do so at a price where there are willing buyers with sufficient funds available to buy it (look at the ask price). This is known as "slippage" or "market impact" and it means that your order may not be filled at the price you initially expected. It can also mean taking a loss if your order isn't filled quickly enough and market conditions change during that time.

How are option prices determined?

As options are derivatives, their price is derived from the asset they are based on. This means that the price of an option is directly proportional to the price of the underlying asset. If you purchase an option that relates to stock trading (e.g. Google stock) then the price will be affected by any fluctuations in the Google share price over time, as well as any major news stories relating to Google. However, there are some additional factors which need to be taken into consideration when determining the price of an option contract:

1. Time value

The time value is a measure of how much the option is worth before it expires. The time value of an option will depend on an array of factors, including:

a. How much time is left until the option expires?
b. What is the volatility of the underlying asset?
c. What current price trend is present in the market for the underlying asset?
d. How far out of the money is the option?

2. Intrinsic value

The intrinsic value is a measure of how much the option is worth if it were to be exercised immediately. The intrinsic value of any option will depend on:

a. The strike price of the option in relation to that of the underlying asset (the greater the difference, the higher the intrinsic value)
b. The current price trend in relation to that of the underlying asset (the greater this difference, the higher the intrinsic value)

The valuation of an option contract

To determine the price of an option, you must take into account its premium, time value and intrinsic value. In this section we will look at how these factors affect the valuation of an option contract. Having a good understanding of this process is essential if you want to be able to trade options successfully.

Valuing an option contract using time value:

In order to calculate the price of an option contract, we need to know three things:

1. The current price of the underlying asset (e.g. Google stock)

2. The strike price of the option (e.g. $1,000)

3. How much time is left until the expiration date for the option (e.g. 3 months)

The premium for any options contract will depend on all three variables listed above and will make up two elements: intrinsic value and time value. Time value will always be relative to how much time is left until expiration, so it makes sense that we should look at these two elements separately before combining them together to find out what the actual price is for any given option contract:

Time value:

The time value will always be relative to the time remaining until expiration and so we need to conduct a second calculation to find out how much time value is being assigned to an option contract.

In our first calculation, we found out that the premium for an option is made up of two elements: intrinsic value and time value. We have already looked at intrinsic value, so we will now look at how time value is determined. To do this, we will use the following formula:

Time Value (T) = Current Price of Underlying Asset (S) x Days to Expiration (T) ÷ Strike Price (K) x Premium per Share (P).

An example of this would be as follows: If you buy a call option on Google stock that expires in 1 month with a strike price of $1,000 and the stock is currently trading at $900, then the premium will be $90 for every share ($900 ÷ $1,000 x 100), with five days left until expiration ($900 ÷ 5). Therefore the Time Value for each share would be 90 x 5 ÷ 1 = 450. This means that your total premium for each share will be made up of $90 in intrinsic value and $450 in time value.

Intrinsic value:

The intrinsic value will always be determined by the strike price of your option contract in relation to that of the underlying asset. If you are long an option, then the higher the premium for an option contract, the more money you will make when it is exercised. However, if you are short an option you will lose money as the premium for an option contract decreases each day until expiration.

To calculate how much intrinsic value is being assigned to a particular call or put option contract, we must use the following formula:

Intrinsic Value (I) = Strike Price (K) x Premium per Share (P) ÷ Current Price of Underlying Asset (S).

For example, if Google stock is trading at $900 and you buy a call with a strike price of $1,000 and 30 days until expiration, then you will receive a premium of $90 per share ($1,000 ÷ $900 x 100). This means that your call has 20 days left until expiration ($900 ÷ 30). Therefore, your intrinsic value for each share will be 920 x 90 ÷ 900 = $80. This means that if you were to exercise your call option contract now, then you would make money as you would only have to pay $900 for a stock that is currently trading at $900. This is because the intrinsic value of your call option contract is greater than the strike price of the underlying asset ($1,000 − $900 = $100).

Valuing an option contract using intrinsic value:

Now that we have established how time value and intrinsic value are calculated separately, we can combine them together to create a complete valuation for an option contract. To do this, we will use the following formula:

Premium per Share (P) = Strike Price (K) x Intrinsic Value (I) ÷ Days until Expiration (T).

This means that when we are valuing an option contract, there are two variables which affect its premium: volatility and days until expiration.

The Risk/Reward of an option contract

Options have a trade-off between the risk and the reward.

If an option trader is bearish about a particular asset he/she can buy a put option which gives him/her the right to sell that particular asset at a specified price. This will be cheaper than actually buying the asset itself as they are saving on the purchase price.

However, buying an option contract has its own risks associated with it. The most significant risk is that if the price of the underlying asset does not fall to meet or equal to that of the strike price, then this could lead to significant losses for them. Another risk is that there is no way to control the price of the underlying asset. They could end up losing a lot of their investment if the price unexpectedly moves in a strong upward direction.

On the other hand, if an investor is bullish about an asset, he/she can buy a call option which gives him/her the right to buy that particular asset at a specified price. This will be more expensive than just buying the underlying asset itself as they are paying more for it. However, buying a call option contract has its own advantages associated with it. The most significant advantage is that if the price of the underlying asset does not rise above or equal to the strike price then this could lead to significant gains for them. Another advantage is that there is no way to control what happens with the underlying asset but they can still profit from their investment because they have paid more for it than what they actually sold it for. For example:

If Apple Inc (NASDAQ:AAPL) stock closes above $120 on January 1st, 2020, then you would be able to sell your AAPL call option contract for $10 each because you had bought them for $5 each but you may or may not get this much money for them. If AAPL stock did not close above $120 then you would be able to sell your call option contract for the original price at which you bought them.

The first example is a bullish scenario for Apple Inc (NASDAQ:AAPL) stock whereas the second one is a bearish scenario.

In both scenarios, there is a risk and there is also an opportunity to make money. The investor should be aware of the trade-off between risk and reward that comes with options contracts and only invest what they can afford to lose.

Chapter 7: Cryptocurrency

The cryptocurrency market is one of the most volatile and risky markets in the world. Deciding on whether to trade cryptocurrency or not can be a hard decision to make. There are many questions to ask yourself before diving into this market. Questions like: Do you have enough money for trading? How much experience do you have in trading? Is it worth it to put all my money into this? Am I prepared for the worst and can I handle a loss?

In this Cryptocurrency chapter, we will answer all your questions regarding Cryptocurrency trading and if it's worth it or not.

What is Cryptocurrency?

Cryptocurrency is a digital currency that allows you to trade online, outside of banks and traditional stock markets.

With cryptocurrency, you can trade, send or receive money without having to go through a bank.

Unlike fiat currency, cryptocurrency is not regulated by any central authority such as the Federal Reserve. Cryptocurrency is completely decentralized which means it's not owned or managed by any country. Every single transaction that occurs on the network is decentralized and open-source which means that no government can control it.

There are some major differences between cryptocurrency and fiat currency. These differences will help you decide if cryptocurrency is right for you or not. Here are some of the major differences:

1. Ownership

With fiat currency, the government owns your money and decides how much money is in circulation. Governments can print as much or as little money as they want. This allows them to control the economy more effectively.

With cryptocurrency, the cryptocurrency is not owned by a government or corporation like it would be with fiat currency. The cryptocurrency is owned by everyone on the network and no one person can control the currency. The entire network of people who own cryptocurrency can decide how much money will be in circulation at any given time.

2. Trust

With fiat currency, you trust the government to give you a certain amount of value for your money through inflation and taxation. Inflation means that your money will buy less later on down the road while taxes decrease your purchasing power even more in a different way than inflation does.

With cryptocurrency, it's important to know that there is no central authority or trusted third-party involved so you will have to trust yourself through self-auditing and making sure that you are keeping proper records of all transactions made on the network. You must also trust other peers on the network to keep their records accurate when sending money between each other. This may seem scary but it's actually safer than using your bank because there are no middlemen with cryptocurrency.

3. Decentralization

With fiat currency, a central authority controls the amount of money in circulation and how it can be transferred or spent. Fiat currency is also regulated by the government which means that they can impose laws on you if you do not follow their rules. This includes laws such as: taxes, inflation, and capital controls.

With cryptocurrency, there is no central authority or government involved so no laws are imposed on you and you don't have to follow any rules to use it. You are completely free to use cryptocurrency however you want without any type of government intervention.

4. Transactions Speed and Fees

With fiat currency, transactions are carried out through a third party service provider or bank that makes sure your transaction goes through safely. These parties charge you fees for each transaction which consists of a percentage of the money being transferred plus a small fee per transaction. With crypto currency, transactions are not carried out through a third party service provider but instead occur directly between two peers on the network without any fees attached to them at all! This is because with cryptocurrency everyone who uses the network pays for maintaining it by donating their computer's processing power to keep everything up and running smoothly. This means that transactions are free and sent instantly to the other party. This is unlike fiat currency where you have to wait days or even weeks for transactions to occur and then you have to pay exorbitant fees for the privilege.

5. Inflation

With fiat currency, inflation is inevitable because there is no limit on the amount of money that can be printed by a central authority. This means that prices will go up over time which makes your money worth less and less and eventually worthless if the government keeps printing too much of it.

With cryptocurrency, there is a limited amount of cryptocurrency that can be in circulation at any given time so there is no inflation! This means that your money will not lose any value over time since supply and demand will remain equal on the network. Once all coins are in circulation, they start losing value which makes it harder for them to be used as a store of value or a currency. For example, once all Bitcoins are mined, they will become almost worthless because as more people mine them the price goes down making it more expensive to use them as a currency since you need more of them to pay for something in comparison with early adopters who only needed one coin to buy something.

6. Government Oversight

With fiat currency, governments can control the economy easily through creating laws and regulations. They can also tax you in any way they want so you have to pay them first before you can spend your money.

With cryptocurrency, there are no taxes or governments involved so you don't have to pay any fees or follow any rules to use it in any way. You are free to use it however you want without any government intervention.

7. Price Stability

With fiat currency, the price is constantly changing based on supply and demand of the market at that time. This means that you never know what your money will buy tomorrow because it's constantly changing in value and demand over time just like stocks do but with stocks, the trend tends to be up over time rather than down over time like fiat currency does. This means that fiat currency is not a good store of value for long term savings because the more money you have in it the less value it will have over long periods of time due to inflation and capital controls by governments which will make it harder for people to get their hands on cash which will decrease demand for goods and services which will push prices down further which makes your money worth less due to deflation over time rather than inflation.

With cryptocurrency, its value does not change over long periods of time because it's a fixed amount that cannot be changed by governments or central authorities. This means that it's a great store of value and can be used as a currency because there is no inflation or deflation which will keep its value over time. If you are looking for a long term investment this is one of the best ways to go since fiat currency will lose most of its value over time due to inflation and capital controls.

8. Government Backing

With fiat currency, the government backs your money so you have to trust them to give you the right amount of money when you exchange it for goods and services. This can be risky because sometimes your money can become worthless due to government regulations and laws such as capital controls etc...

With cryptocurrency, there is no central authority or government involved so you don't have to trust anyone with your money. It's completely decentralized and every transaction can be seen on the network so you know that everyone involved in the transaction has nothing to hide from you which makes the network more trustworthy than using your bank where all transactions are hidden from you which leaves room for fraud and scams since there are middlemen involved with fiat currency.

9. Transferring Money

With fiat currency, you have to go through a third party service provider or bank to transfer money since they control the flow of money and make sure everything is going smoothly. With cryptocurrency, you can transfer money directly from peer to peer without having to deal with any middlemen. This means that there is no one between you and the person you are sending your money to which increases security and decreases fraud and scams since middlemen are involved with fiat currency. The only time middlemen are involved is when you exchange your cryptocurrency for fiat currency in order to buy something with it outside of the network or trade it for another cryptocurrency.

10. Privacy

With fiat currency, all transactions are tracked by the government since they control where the money goes so your activity can be monitored and analyzed by them in order to keep an eye on what everyone is doing in case someone is doing something suspicious or criminal like tax evasion or fraud etc... This gives governments an excuse to keep tabs on everyone's activities without getting anyone's consent which makes it easier for them to do bad things against their citizens like spying on them, tracking their movements, arresting them based on false accusations etc... The privacy of citizens becomes compromised because of all this.

With cryptocurrency, privacy is provided by the network because all transactions are decentralized and every transaction is visible on the network so no one can trace where your money went or came from unless you add a personal touch to it which most people don't. This gives you full control over your activity and allows you to do whatever you want without anyone tracking or knowing what you are doing since it's not visible on the network like fiat currency where anything can be tracked once someone has access to the data.

11. Government Intervention

With fiat currency, the government can decide to intervene and change the value of your money without letting you know about it. This usually happens in times of crisis such as economic crises or wars etc... where they need more money to help cover their expenses. This means that your money can become worthless in a matter of seconds if the government decides to intervene with it which makes fiat currency extremely risky as a tradable asset.

With cryptocurrency, governments cannot intervene since it's decentralized and not owned by any nation. This means that no one can change how much your cryptocurrency is worth which makes it a lot safer than fiat currency when you look at the potential risks that come along with using it.

The different types of cryptocurrencies

There are over 1,500 different types of cryptocurrencies available on the internet. Each one of them has its own set of rules and regulations, which vary from one cryptocurrency to another. However, the most popular ones are Ethereum, Bitcoin, Litecoin, Ripple and Dash.

Here are some of the most popular cryptocurrencies:

1. Bitcoin

Bitcoin is the most popular cryptocurrency, and it was created by an anonymous person who goes by the name of Satoshi Nakamoto. This is a digital currency that uses peer-to-peer technology to operate with no central authority or banks.

2. Litecoin

Litecoin was created by Charlie Lee, a former Google employee, in 2011 as an alternative to Bitcoin. It improves upon Bitcoin by using a different type of Cryptographic algorithm called Scrypt, which makes mining Litecoins easier as compared to Bitcoins. Also, Litecoin has a faster block generation rate than that of Bitcoins (a block is created every 2.5 minutes), and it also has more coins in circulation than the former cryptocurrency (84 million).

3. Ethereum (ETH)

Ethereum was created in 2013 by Vitalik Buterin, and it operates on a blockchain just like Bitcoin and Litecoin do. However, its underlying technology allows for applications to be built on top of it which supports smart contracts at its core as well as having its own currency called ethers. The smart contracts allow for enforcement of agreements as well as transparency between users within the network without any outside interference from any third party.

4. Dash (DASH)

Dash was created in 2014 by Evan Duffield, and it is a cryptocurrency that uses a two-tier architecture consisting of miners and masternodes. The miners are in charge of confirming transactions, while the masternodes include individuals that can provide services to other users within the network, such as privacy and instant transactions. Dash is also used for so-called "instant transactions" as well as having a type of built-in governance system that allows users to vote on features they want to be added or removed from the system.

5. Ripple (XRP)

Ripple was created in 2012 by Jed McCaleb and Chris Larsen and it is a real-time gross settlement protocol that is currency agnostic. In other words, Ripple works with every currency and doesn't discriminate between them. Also, it allows people to freely trade any currency in the world without any charges or fees involved.

6. NEO (NEO)

NEO was created by Onchain (formerly Antshares) in 2014, but it was rebranded in 2017 after a complete revamp of its original blockchain codebase and operating systems. It is similar to Ethereum in many ways including its smart contracts, but its focus is on digital assets stored on smart contracts rather than just being used for financial transactions within its network like Ethereum does with Ether.

7. Binance Coin (BNB)

Binance Coin was created in 2017 by Changpeng Zhao, and it is the official cryptocurrency of Finance, which is a popular cryptocurrency exchange platform. The purpose of Binance Coin is to be used as a means of payment on the platform itself.

8. Stellar (XLM)

Stellar was created in 2014 by Jed McCaleb, and it aims to connect banks, payment systems and people together through its decentralized network. It connects people from any corner of the globe through its distributed ledger technology and consensus mechanism. It also allows people to send money across borders quickly and at no cost while also being able to track its transaction history at any time.

9. Litecoin Cash (LCC)

Litecoin Cash was released on February 20th, 2018 by an anonymous individual or a group of individuals who call themselves "Team Rocket". The main reason behind this new cryptocurrency is for it to have faster transactions than that of Litecoin, which have been growing slower over time due to more people using this coin for transactions rather than just for mining purposes. Moreover, Litecoin Cash has even faster blocks than that of Litecoins' 2.5 minutes per block.

10. Dashcoin (DSH)

Dashcoin was created in 2013 by Evan Duffield, and it has similarities to that of the previously mentioned Dash cryptocurrency. However, unlike Dash, Dashcoin doesn't use masternodes or Proof-of-Work (PoW) at its core. Instead, it uses a custom protocol called X11 based on the original Bitcoin protocol to secure its network.

11. Ethereum Classic (ETC)

Ethereum Classic was created as a hard fork of Ethereum in 2016 after the DAO hack. The fork happened because there was a disagreement within the community over how to handle the hack on the original blockchain system that created this cryptocurrency in the first place. There was a second hard fork of Ethereum Classic that took place in 2017 which changed its consensus mechanism from Proof-of-Work to Proof-of-Stake – this change was done to avoid ASIC mining rigs from being used on its blockchain network as they were being used for mining purposes on other cryptocurrencies such as Monero and Bitcoin Gold at this time.

12. Monero (XMR)

Monero is another cryptocurrency that was created in 2014 by an anonymous individual or group of individuals. It uses Proof-of-Work (PoW) to secure its network, and it is also one of the most popular privacy-focused cryptocurrencies on the market.

13. Zcash (ZEC)

Zcash was created in 2016 by Zooko Wilcox, and it uses a different type of cryptography than that of Bitcoin's SHA256, which makes it more secure than Bitcoin as well as being able to support confidential transactions between users within its network. It has been improved upon by its developers over time, which has led to its current position among other cryptocurrencies out there today since this was one of the first cryptocurrencies to have a strong focus on privacy and anonymity of transactions.

14. Bitcoin Cash (BCH)

Bitcoin Cash is a hard fork of Bitcoin, which was created on August 1st, 2017. It features new opcodes as well as the integration of SegWit, and also removes the need for an extra block in the blockchain to be used as a free transaction block. It also has replay and wipeout protection, which means that this cryptocurrency can be used safely even if it comes into contact with the Bitcoin blockchain. However, it should be noted that Bitcoin Cash is not compatible with all wallets because they may not support this cryptocurrency's transaction format.

How was cryptocurrencies created?

In 2008, an individual or group known by the pseudonym Satoshi Nakamoto published a white paper titled "Bitcoin: A Peer-to-Peer Electronic Cash System". In 2009, they released software that implements that idea, and created the network now known as Bitcoin. The first Bitcoin specification and proof of concept was published in 2009 in a cryptography mailing list by Satoshi Nakamoto.

The Bitcoin protocol was officially released in January of 2009 by Satoshi Nakamoto and others. Within the first two months (February) of that year, over 1 million bitcoin had been mined which is worth almost $17 billion at today's value. This amount was reduced to 25% of its original value in June 2014.

The word bitcoin was first used and defined in a white paper published on 31 October 2008. The author is believed to be Satoshi Nakamoto.

In September 2011 Vitalik Buterin co-founded Bitcoin Magazine. In December he released a paper describing Ethereum. In January 2014, he released the Ethereum software development kit, which enabled developers to build their own applications on top of the Ethereum platform. Buterin had argued that Bitcoin needed a scripting language for application development. Failing to gain agreement, he proposed development of a new platform with a more general scripting language.

In February 2014, Buterin released a much anticipated white paper describing Ethereum. In 2014, Ethereum had launched a pre-sale for ether which received an overwhelming response; this allowed the Ethereum project to receive funding of $18 million in a few days before its launch.

By July 2015, the word "Ethereum" was ranked #1 by Google in the most searched keywords. In the same month, it was announced that over $11 million worth of ether was sold in the first five days of its launch. The Ethereum network went live on 30th July 2015 and the first GAS (GAS is what powers Ethereum) were mined in August 2015.

The Categories of Cryptocurrencies

1. Centralized cryptocurrencies

This type of cryptocurrencies is governed by a central bank and they control the supply of money. These cryptocurrencies are created by a government or a bank and can be printed out to meet the needs of the economy. These types of cryptocurrencies are used in everyday transactions, just like fiat currency (USD, EURO, GBP etc.).

For example, Ripple is a centralized cryptocurrency that is being used by several banks.

2. Decentralized cryptocurrencies

This type of cryptocurrency is not governed by any central body and is created according to the terms of its blockchain (a public ledger of all transactions in the network). Since these cryptocurrencies are not governed they are completely decentralized, which means that they have limited or no interference from any governing body. In this type of cryptocurrency, there will be no involvement from banks or any other financial institutions. This is a good thing because it eliminates the need for third parties to approve transactions and also eliminates fees associated with them.

The main advantage of using decentralized cryptocurrencies is anonymity and privacy, as well as no interference from governing bodies like banks, government etc. The customer does not have to worry about their details being shared with a third party because there are no third parties involved in these transactions. These types of cryptocurrencies are mostly used in online payments and other day-to-day transactions such as buying coffee at your local Starbucks shop etc.

Decentralized cryptocurrencies can be classified into two types:

1. Proof of Work (PoW)

In a PoW system, miners solve a cryptographic puzzle to validate a transaction and add it to the blockchain. The process of mining is called proof of work because it is an expensive computational resource that requires a high amount of electricity and hardware to solve the puzzle. The miner who solves the puzzle first gets rewarded with new coins, which in this case are Bitcoin. This type of cryptocurrency has become quite popular in recent times because they are not governed by any central bank or financial institutions, which makes them extremely popular among those who prefer a decentralized system over centralized systems.

The major disadvantage of using PoW systems is that they require vast amounts of electricity and computational power to confirm transactions, which makes them less efficient than PoS cryptocurrencies. Another disadvantage is that the amount of energy used to create these cryptocurrencies can be very high, which causes environmental pollution and increases electricity costs for everyone else in the network as well.

2. Proof of Stake (PoS)

In a PoS system, users who own coins in their wallet can mine or validate transactions by sending coins from their wallet to themselves as transaction fees. The idea is that the more coins you hold in your wallet, the more "interest" you will generate. This type of cryptocurrency is very efficient because it requires very little computational power and much less electricity.

The primary disadvantage of a PoS consensus mechanism is that they are susceptible to centralization because only those who have a large number of coins in their wallet can participate in transactions. PoS systems also pose the risk of coin holders trying to double spend coins or create new coins; this means they can basically create money out of thin air, which is a major problem with these types of cryptocurrencies.

What determines the price of a cryptocurrency?

Although there is no single answer to that question, it is safe to say that it is a combination of the following:

1. Supply and demand

Firstly, most cryptocurrencies are decentralized. This means that there is no central bank controlling the supply and demand of the cryptocurrency. The number of coins that are created by mining or created during an ICO (Initial Coin Offering) is set at the time the currency was created. Thus, supply and demand determine what the price will be.

Also, most cryptocurrencies have a fixed supply. This means that there is only a specific number of coins in circulation. This is unlike fiat currencies which have the ability to be printed at will.

2. Speculation

Secondly, the price of a cryptocurrency is also affected by speculation. Just like any other currency, people tend to speculate on what the price of a cryptocurrency will be in the future. If people think that a certain coin will increase in value, they are likely to buy it and hold on to it for the long-term – thus increasing its value.

3. Government intervention

Lastly, governments can have an impact on the price of cryptocurrencies by regulating them or banning them altogether. They can do this through various means ranging from media censorship to actually creating regulations for cryptocurrencies within their country's borders (or even globally). Some governments have banned cryptocurrencies because of concerns over money laundering and other illegal activities that can take place with these currencies. Of course, you should always do your research before investing in any type of cryptocurrency as not all countries tolerate cryptocurrencies equally!

4. Institutional investors

Moreover, institutional investors such as hedge funds and banks are starting to invest in cryptocurrencies. This is because of the fact that they believe that some cryptocurrencies will become part of the financial mainstream in the future (similar to how stocks are traded today). These institutional investors have a significant amount of money to invest as well, which can cause a significant impact on their currency prices.

6. Mining

In order to create new coins, people have to mine for them. Mining is a process that requires the computer to solve complex mathematical problems for which they are rewarded with new coins. This process requires a lot of power, and hence those who can afford better mining equipment will be able to mine more coins than those who cannot afford such equipment. Mining also plays an important role in the security of the cryptocurrency as it prevents fraudulent transactions from taking place.

7. Exchanges

Exchanges such as Coinbase or Binance play a role in the price of a cryptocurrency. Users of these exchanges can purchase cryptocurrencies by exchanging their fiat currency such as USD or EUR for the cryptocurrency. However, the price of cryptocurrencies on most exchanges is usually different from the price directly from the coin creators because of fees and other things.

8. Forks or Hard Forks

Sometimes, a hard fork is created from an existing cryptocurrency. A hard fork is when the developers of a cryptocurrency change the code of the blockchain in order to create a new cryptocurrency. This can happen when there is a disagreement between developers about how to move forward with that currency. The new cryptocurrency created after this fork will then be traded on the existing exchanges as well as having its own unique price.

9. Other Cryptocurrencies

The value of most cryptocurrencies are affected by other cryptocurrencies. When one cryptocurrency rises in value, it will affect the price of other cryptocurrencies due to market forces which push and pull demand between currencies based on their relative values. This was most noticeable with Bitcoin when it jumped to $19,000 per coin in December 2017 – this caused a significant rally in other cryptocurrencies which was known as the "Crypto-Mania".

The risk/return of trading cryptocurrencies

Cryptocurrencies are almost a synonym for volatility. For most of their short history, the price of cryptocurrencies has fluctuated wildly. Like a super-volatile stock, if you know what you're doing, trading cryptocurrencies can be a great way to make a lot of money in a short time. But it can also be incredibly risky and there is a substantial amount of risk in trading cryptocurrencies. If you are not careful, you could end up losing all of your money or worse.

Most retail traders are speculators in the sense that they're not buying cryptocurrencies for medium term trading, but rather to make a quick buck through rapid and risky price movements; for example, the price of a cryptocurrency may double from one day to the next. If you are going to trade cryptocurrencies, you must have an exit strategy in place.

There are some cryptocurrency online trading platforms that offer you leverage, so that you will be able to trade on a larger scale. This can lead to some significant profits in the short run, but it can also lead to some big losses if you are not careful.

There are many individuals who have made a fortune of a lifetime by taking advantage of fast-moving cryptocurrencies. However, there are also many individuals who have made a lot of money in a short amount of time; then lost all the money in an even shorter amount of time. If you are going to trade cryptocurrencies, you need to be prepared for these types of surprises.

Cryptocurrency trading is not for the layman or for people who do not know the basics about stocks, forex or futures trading and have never traded before. You are likely to lose all your money if you do not know what you're doing and this is particularly true when trading cryptocurrencies. If you do decide to trade cryptocurrencies, there is a 90% chance that you will lose all your money.

To avoid mistakes that could cost you dearly, make sure that you understand what an ICO (Initial Coin Offering) is before investing in one and make sure that you are comfortable with crypto exchanges, crypto wallets and cryptocurrency news sites before starting to invest.

There will be a lot of scammers out there selling overvalued assets and if you cannot tell the difference between real value and fake value then chances are high that your investment will be worthless.

If you are going to trade cryptocurrencies, you must have a plan in place before you start trading.

What is an ICO?

The acronym 'ICO' is for 'Initial Coin Offering'. An ICO is when a company issues their own currency across the blockchain.

An example of this is how Ethereum was a successful ICO. They released their own cryptocurrency called Ether, that can be used to pay for services and transaction fees on the Ethereum blockchain.

This can be compared with an IPO (Initial Public Offering) which is when companies list on the stock market, and offer shares in order to raise money for their business.

Retail traders like yourself can participate in ICOs because you can purchase these tokens for a cheaper price than if you were to buy the token after it had been listed on a cryptocurrency exchange.

This is because the company that is raising the funds is selling off their own currency at a dirt cheap price in order to raise money for their business.

What is a Crypto Wallet?

A crypto wallet is a digital application that allows you to make digital transactions. It stores your public and private keys which allow you to send and receive cryptocurrencies.

Crypto wallets are also known as cryptocurrency wallets or digital wallets. The main difference between these two is the fact that a digital wallet can be used for fiat currencies as well as cryptocurrencies, while cryptocurrency wallets only allow you to store your cryptocurrencies on them. Digital wallets are also known as online wallets, mobile wallets or web-based wallets.

There are different types of crypto/digital/cryptocurrency/cryptocurrency wallets depending on how they are built, how secure they are, the amount of coins they support and their location (online vs offline). For example: mobile phones, desktop computers, hardware devices like USBs, servers with private keys or just storage in your brain (memorizing passwords).

To protect your crypto wallet from hackers or scammers there are several security measures you can take such as adding multiple security layers to your online platform such as 2FA (2 Factor Authentication), password requirements for purchases etc. These methods greatly improve the safety of your crypto wallet but aren't 100% foolproof and might still cause you some problems.

Most cryptocurrency online trading platforms like Binance, Coinbase and Kraken offer you to store your private keys online on their websites. Such platforms are usually very secure and are regularly checked by security experts but if you don't trust the platform or online services you can always store your keys offline in a hardware wallet.

A hardware wallet is a physical device that stores encrypted data on it. This is an offline solution that separates your public and private keys from the internet and makes them impossible to hack. There are several brands of hardware wallets available such as Ledger Nano S, Trezor, KeepKey and Digital BitBox.

How to trade Cryptocurrency

1. Open a cryptocurrency account with an exchange.

First, decide on the cryptocurrency online trading platform with the most favourable fees and liquidity. There are many platforms to choose from. Once when you have decided, open an account by filling out the registration form. Usually, most firms will require you to perform a short Know-Your-Customer procedure before you can start trading. This involves uploading your ID and proof of residence.

2. Verify your account

The security of your account is important, you will likely be required to verify your identity before being allowed to deposit or withdraw money. Some exchanges allow you to trade without verification, but most will require you to go through the process. This can vary depending on the country you live in and is usually supported by a bank account or a credit/debit card.

3. Deposit funds into your new account.

Deposits are usually done via bank transfer, credit/debit card, or even a cryptocurrency itself. The fees will vary depending on the payment method and the currency used. Some exchanges support only one or two payment methods while others will accept just about any major credit card.

4. Start trading!

Now that you have your account and money in it let's begin trading! The process of buying and selling Cryptocurrencies is really simple. All you need to do is to click on the 'Buy' or 'Sell' button, depending on which one you want to do, choose the amount of the cryptocurrency you want to trade, and then enter the price and amount you wish to buy or sell.

5. Sell your cryptocurrency on an online market.

Once you have bought your cryptocurrency it is time to sell it again! Most exchanges will allow you to sell your cryptocurrency back for a credit card, bank transfer, or some other type of currency such as US dollars. You can also directly withdraw funds into your bank account without any fees or charges!

6. Transfer your cryptocurrency to a stable coin

If you want to convert your cryptocurrency into a stable coin such as Tether, Decred or Tron, you will need to send it to a cryptocurrency exchange that supports such coins.

The trading process for a stable coin is the same as for any other cryptocurrency. You place an order on the exchange of your choice and wait until someone buys it. Once the transaction is complete, the money will be available in your account and you can transfer it to your wallet.

Using stable coins is a good way to avoid losses from the volatility of the cryptocurrency market as it is almost the same as converting your cryptocurrency into fiat currency, as most of the stable coins are pegged to the US dollar.

7. Transfer cryptocurrency to your crypto wallet (Optional)

Since most exchanges don't allow you to withdraw money directly to your bank account, you will need to transfer the funds to your crypto wallet. Usually, an exchange will allow you to withdraw funds only when you have a certain amount of cryptocurrency on your account. So it is recommendable that if you are planning on withdrawing any sum of money that is greater than $5,000, you should withdraw the money in chunks of $5,000 or less.

Why is cryptocurrency growing so fast?

Cryptocurrency is growing so fast and the reason for that is that people are starting to realize what can be done with it. When cryptocurrencies were first created, they were designed to facilitate economic transactions in a decentralized and anonymous manner.

The blockchain technology that cryptocurrencies use allows for the secure and transparent transfer of money without a third party, like a bank, being involved. Also, the protocol behind cryptocurrency transactions is public knowledge because it's on an open ledger. You can see every transaction that's ever been made from one cryptocurrency to another so there's no hiding or manipulating data related to cryptocurrency transfers. So if you look at those two things alone, you can see why cryptocurrencies are becoming such a useful tool in today's society.

What are the positive aspects of cryptocurrency?

As mentioned above, cryptocurrencies have many benefits over traditional currency. The first thing we want to look at is how secure cryptocurrency is compared with other forms of money. Cryptocurrencies use encryption techniques to control the creation of new units, verify transactions and prevent double-spending when you send the same coin to two different recipients (this process also confirms your personal identity). This system makes it almost impossible for your crypto to be stolen by anybody.

Another positive aspect of cryptocurrencies is that you get full control of your funds. It's in your hands to send your cryptocurrency to any address you want, and you can do so anonymously. This means you're also able to keep your financial information private and secure, which is a big plus for anyone who values their privacy.

The freedom that cryptocurrencies give you is also a big reason why they're becoming so popular so fast. The blockchain technology behind most cryptocurrencies eliminates the need for banks when it comes to transferring money from one person to another. Banks are still needed in the initial stages of cryptocurrency transactions but once the transaction has been made, there's no need for a middleman anymore because it can be verified on the blockchain ledger itself.

This has created a lot of small business owners who have decided not to use banks anymore to transfer money but rather use cryptocurrency because it's cheaper and much faster than using banks for transfers. Startups are particularly fond of cryptocurrency because they don't have access to big bank loans or venture capital funding like larger businesses do, so they have an easier time raising capital when starting out if they decide to use cryptocurrency.

What are the negative aspects of cryptocurrency?

The biggest problem with cryptocurrencies is that there's no real regulation or oversight. It's possible for anyone to start their own cryptocurrency and find ways to scam people out of their money. In fact, this happened in the past when a group of people created a new cryptocurrency called Paycoin and claimed it would be backed by gold (which wasn't true). They made a lot of money from investors who believed them, but once they realized this was a scam, they got their money back. However, these investors lost big time because the creators of Paycoin kept most of the money for themselves.

Because there's been so many scams like that in the past, it's very important to treat every cryptocurrency you come across as a potential scam until proven otherwise. Do your research before investing in any cryptocurrency because if you don't do that and you lose your money, it will be hard to get it back once you realize you were scammed.

Another potential risk with cryptocurrencies is that there's currently not enough places to use them for everyday transactions like buying goods and services. Most businesses still prefer dealing in fiat currency and not cryptocurrency, so you're mostly limited to using cryptocurrencies to transfer money from one person to another.

Today, cryptocurrency has found mainstream adoption in places like Japan and South Korea, where some businesses accept cryptocurrency as a form of payment. However, it's still not the norm. So this is another drawback of cryptocurrency because most people will not be able to pay for their day-to-day needs with cryptocurrency for a long time.

Chapter 8: Strategies and Tips

Now that we have covered all the financial instruments that you can trade in this book, it is time to talk about the right way to start trading. In this chapter, we will give you the best strategies and tips that you can use to get started on your trading journey.

When is the best time to trade?

Most people will tell you that there is no perfect time to trade. This is true to a certain extent, but there are some times when you can have an advantage over the market.

The best time to trade is when you have an edge over the market. Usually, this means that you should be trading on a market that you know very well or have done research on.

If you are not trading on a free or demo account, then I would suggest that you do not trade on a stock that you do not understand well enough. If this is what your strategy is, then by all means, go ahead and start placing trades on stocks that are in your portfolio. However, I am going to warn you now that it will not work for long and will cost you quite a bit of money if it does work at all.

By using this strategy, I am going to assume that most people are going to start with forex trading and cryptocurrencies at least until they are able to learn more about the other markets. Either way, the best way for beginners to learn about trading is through practice by using a demo account or paper trading until they feel confident enough in their abilities to start risking their own money in their trades.

The best time to trade is when you have a good understanding of what you are trading and have a strategy that will give you an edge over the market. You will know if your strategy has an edge over the market if it makes money more often than it loses money and also by how much money you are making in profit on each trade. The higher your win rate, the better. The more money that you can make per trade, the better. If you can find a strategy that gives you both then that is the best of all worlds and what I would recommend.

However, this is not always possible and many times people need to start with a strategy that they know will let them make some money even if it is not necessarily the most profitable one available to them.

The best time to start trading would be when there is some kind of event happening in the market that will cause prices to change by at least a couple of points in either direction in order for your strategies to be able to be used effectively. This could be something as simple as a major economic report coming out or news about a company's quarterly earnings report being released. Of course, there are other things like holidays or newsworthy events but those are much more difficult to predict and will be covered in the next chapter.

As a general rule, the best time to trade is when you have an edge over the market. If you do not have an edge over the market then it would be better for you to wait until you can find one instead of trading blindly with your own money.

What are the different trading strategies?

There are many trading strategies that you can use and we are going to cover some of the best ones here.

1. Scalper Trading:

This is the first strategy that most people learn about. Scalping is a trading strategy where you hope to find small price discrepancies in the market and make quick trades. The reason for this is to make small profits on every trade that you make. That way, in order to end up with a big profit, you will only need to win a few trades and this strategy allows you to do that. The opposite of this kind of strategy would be swing trading which requires holding positions for longer periods of time.

For example, if you are trading on Bitcoin, then you will have to try and find a price difference of around 1% between the lowest and highest price that Bitcoin has reached in the last hour. If such a price difference exists, then you will be able to make an easy trade by buying when the lowest point is reached and selling when the highest point is reached.

2. Trend Following:

This is a strategy that works best with stocks and forex. It is a strategy that is based on the idea that you will buy when the market is going up and sell when it is going down. Many traders claim that this strategy works best when you are willing to wait until the market has already bottomed out before selling.

For example, if you are trading stocks, then you will need to wait until the market has already bottomed out and is going up again before selling. This way, you will end up with a large profit. The opposite of this kind of strategy would be the counter-trading which involves buying when the market is going down and selling when it is going up.

3. Arbitrage:

This is another strategy that mostly works with stock trading. With this strategy, you try to find different prices of the same stock in different markets around the world and buy from the cheapest one and sell in the most expensive one. This way, you can earn a quick profit without having to wait for too long for your trade to end.

An example would be if you are trading stocks and you come across a stock that is trading at $100 in one place and $110 in another. You will buy from the one that is $100 and sell in the one that is $110. This way, you will earn a quick profit without having to wait for too long for your trade to end.

4. Trendline Trading:

This strategy involves following the trend lines on charts. This strategy works by following a trend line, buying when it goes up and selling when it goes down. It only works best with stock trading because other financial instruments don't have lines on their charts. This strategy can be used with both counter-trading and trend following strategies because it involves choosing which direction the market is going in before buying or selling.

For example, if you are trading stocks, then you will need to choose whether or not the market is going up before buying any stocks or not. If it is going down, then you need to sell all your stocks before they are worth less than what they were before. That way, this strategy allows you to use both counter-trading and trend following strategies together in order to make more money in less time.

5. Intraday Trading:

This is another strategy that works well with stocks. This is a strategy that involves buying and selling stocks on the same day. Many people think that you can't make money with this kind of strategy because it requires you to pay a lot of fees and many brokers don't allow you to move your trades around every day. However, there are also ways to avoid such fees, and it can be quite profitable if you do it right. This strategy is not a good one for other financial instruments because they don't move as quickly as stocks do.

For example, if you are trading stocks, then you will have to buy when the price goes down or sell when the price goes up. You will also have to sell when the price reaches a certain amount before moving on to a different trade. This way, this kind of strategy allows you to take advantage of trends within one day but also move on quickly if they turn out not to be profitable.

How can technical analysis be used in conjunction with fundamental analysis?

This is a question that we are often asked and the answer is quite simple. We believe that technical analysis can be used in conjunction with fundamental analysis. That's because technical analysis provides you with more information about the price of a financial instrument. More information is always good when it comes to trading.

The only type of person that should not use technical analysis is a person that has no idea what they are doing. If you do not know what you are doing, technical analysis will just give you more information on which financial instruments to avoid and which ones to buy.

Therefore, it is important that you understand the basics of technical analysis before you start using it. You can learn all about the basics in this book. Once you have done that, it will be much easier for you to use technical analysis in conjunction with fundamental analysis.

What do we mean by "in conjunction with"? We mean after performing fundamental analysis on a certain security, if we see prices increasing or decreasing at a faster rate than what the fundamentals predict, then we could use technical analysis to confirm our opinion about the investment opportunity. Or if we do not have any opinion about an investment opportunity and we just want to invest in something that is priced below its fair market value, then we could use technical analysis to figure out whether or not this price difference is sustainable for a certain period of time.

The choice is yours but always remember that using both fundamental and technical analyses together will give you a better chance of earning profits in the long term.

In order to use both fundamental and technical analyses together, you will need to have a good understanding of both technical and fundamental analysis. Here are some tips that you can use to better understand both types of analysis.

1. Learn the basics of technical analysis first.

It is important that you know how to use technical analysis and how it works first. There are many things that you will need to learn about technical analysis, such as the various chart patterns that can be used to predict the future price movements of a security. Once you have learned all about the basics, then you will be able to use technical analysis in conjunction with fundamental analysis.

Technical analysis is useful to know when the right time is to buy or sell certain financial instruments. However, it is also very useful when it comes to determining the best entry and exit points when trading a certain financial instrument. Usually, the best way to find these entry and exit points is by using technical analysis.

2. Understand what fundamental analysis is all about.

You can learn about fundamental analysis in this book. While you only need a basic understanding of fundamental analysis to use it in conjunction with technical analysis, you should have a complete understanding of it before you start trading on your own. That's because not all financial instruments are affected by fundamental analysis in the same way and you will need to know how each financial instrument reacts or does not react to changes in fundamentals.

For example, if the price of gold goes up, then you should expect that gold mining stocks will go down in price because their profit margins will become smaller due to increased operational costs due to higher prices for things like electricity and labor. Plus, gold will likely go up even more if the global economy remains stable and inflation stays low since there are fewer gold mines than there are other businesses that need supplies from around the world which causes supply chains to become very tight when demand increases causing prices for many commodities to go up.

On the other hand, if the price of gold goes down, then you should expect the price of gold mining stocks to go up in price since their profit margins will increase. However, if there is a major natural disaster or war that causes supply chains to become more effective, then you should expect the price of gold mining stocks to go down because there will be less demand for them from worldwide buyers. This is because they will be able to find alternative sources of gold which are much cheaper than gold mining stocks.

3. Learn how these two disciplines can be used in conjunction with one another.

Once you have covered the basics of fundamental analysis and technical analysis, it will be much easier for you to use them together to make better trading decisions. This is because once you know how both disciplines work, then it will be much easier to combine the two disciplines in order to create a trading strategy that works for your unique situation.

4. Avoid using emotions when making trading decisions.

Emotions are the enemy of all traders and investors out there. It is very easy to make trading decisions based on emotions alone without thinking rationally about the decision that you are making at the time. It is important that you think rationally when making these types of decisions so that your emotions do not get in the way of your decision-making process.

5. Do not trade excessively or too frequently.

The purpose of this book is not to tell you how much money you can make if you trade excessively or too frequently but we do need to tell you this important piece of advice on how not to lose a lot of money from excessive trading more than anything else because it can be very tempting sometimes when there is so much money to be made if only we spend more time at the trading terminal.

The problem with excessive trading is that it will cause you to make more mistakes than if you were to trade less often because you have less time to make a mistake. That's because the more time you spend at your trading terminal, the higher your risk of making a mistake is which will cause you to lose money if you are trading in an instrument that goes down when the fundamentals predict that it should go up or if it goes up when the fundamentals predict that it should go down.

The best way to avoid excessive trading is to have a trading strategy in place before entering into a trade. This way, you will not be tempted to make more trades than what your strategy calls for and therefore, avoid making unnecessary mistakes by being excessively active with your trading.

What is your Risk Profile?

This is the first question that you need to ask yourself when you start trading. This is because it will change the type of strategy that you will use. There are three different risk profiles:

1. Conservative

Those that have a conservative risk profile are the ones that are not willing to risk a lot of their capital in trading. This is because they want to avoid having substantial losses on their accounts. This is because they are not willing to take any unnecessary risks with their capital.

These traders will use strategies that are primarily conservative and only use a small portion of their capital for trading. This is because the trades will require minimal capital in order to deliver a decent profit. Most of the time, they will use no more than 1-4% of their total capital for trading at any given time.

The common conservative choice of trading is to use a buy and hold strategy. This means that you will buy an asset and then hold on to it until it reaches its peak value. Once it peaks, you will sell it for a profit.

The best types of financial instruments for you are the ones that have a good growth potential but are not too risky. You can use the 60/40 asset allocation model to achieve this. In this model, you will allocate 60% of your total capital for low-risk investments, and 40% will go to high-risk investments. Bonds and dividend stocks are low-risk options, while cryptocurrencies are high-risk.

2. Moderate

Those with a moderate risk profile are willing to take higher risks with their investments. This is because they have more capital and better risk management skills than the conservative investors.

These investors are not willing to lose all of their capital in a trade, but they know that taking risks is necessary in order to make the most of their trading activities.

The common type of strategy that high-risk traders use is called scalping. The scalping strategy basically involves buying and selling assets within a short period of time. This is done to take advantage of the short-term price fluctuations of an asset.

3. Aggressive

Those with an aggressive risk profile can afford to lose a large amount of their capital in a trade. This is because they have more capital and better risk management skills than the moderate investors. They are willing to take risks with their investments because they know that it is possible to make large profits using this strategy.

If you want to trade like an aggressive investor, then you should use a day-trading strategy with leverage. In this strategy, you will buy and sell assets within the same trading day (i.e., within one day). The idea behind this is to buy low and sell high when the prices fluctuate on a daily basis (or even hourly basis). You can use a margin account for this, which will allow you to buy more assets than your total capital would usually allow.

The most aggressive types of financial instruments are the most volatile, such as cryptocurrencies and Forex. This is because these instruments are very sensitive to the daily news flow and market sentiment.

Whether you choose to be conservative or aggressive, it is important to remember that every investor has a different risk profile. No matter what your risk profile is, make sure you learn how to manage your risks in the best way possible.

What is Your Time Frame:

This is the second question that you need to ask yourself when you start trading. It will determine which strategy fits best for your trading activities. There are three types of time frames:

1. Short term

This strategy involves holding an asset for less than one month before selling it for a profit or loss. Many of the strategies that we have discussed so far fall into this category, including day-trading and swing trading strategies (only if they involve short-term holding periods). This means that you will be buying and selling assets within a month's time frame. These strategies require a lot of active monitoring on your part because you will need to know when to buy and sell at the right time.

2. Medium term

This strategy involves holding an asset for more than one month but less than one year before selling it for a profit or loss. Many of the strategies that we have discussed so far fall into this category, including position trading, swing trading, and timing trading strategies. This means that you will be buying and selling assets within a year's time frame. You will have to monitor your trades in order to get the best returns on investment.

3. Long term

This strategy involves holding an asset for more than one year before selling it for a profit or loss. This means that you will be buying and selling assets within three years' time frame. You have to be more risk tolerant in order to succeed in this type of trading because you have a longer period of time to wait before reaping the benefits of your investments. It requires a more passive approach than the previous two time frames.

The best investment strategies are the ones that fit the time frame of your available activities. If you are a busy person who has no time for active monitoring, then you should stick to investing for a long period of time frame. It will require a lot of patience, but it will give you better results in the end.

Conclusion

As the saying goes, "a rising tide lifts all boats", and the same applies to markets when there is a bull market. The market has undergone a massive correction which has shaken a lot of people's confidence in the markets, especially those who are new to trading.

Investing is all about managing your risk and your emotions. It can be a very daunting experience for a beginner to begin trading. There is a lot of information out there, much of which is conflicting and confusing. It will definitely take time to accumulate enough knowledge in order to make the right decisions. With that said, trading and investing are not for everyone. It takes courage, hard work and a lot of time. As long as you have the patience and perseverance, trading is not something that should be taken lightly.

In order to be successful in trading, you need to be willing to put in the time and effort into learning the craft. One of the most important things is to find a trading style that makes sense for your personality. Not all styles will fit your personality, therefore it is important to experiment until you find a style that fits your personality.

The most important thing to remember is that trading is not a get rich quick scheme! You have to be willing to lose a lot of money at the beginning in order to learn the necessary skills.

Finally, always remember that even the best traders get 50% of their trades wrong. This is not because they are bad traders, but because it is impossible to know where the market will go next. The best traders are the ones who are not always right, but the ones who have found ways to accept that they will be wrong quite often.

Thank you again for reading!

www.ingramcontent.com/pod-product-compliance
Lightning Source LLC
Chambersburg PA
CBHW071410210526
45465CB00001B/329